# INSIDE Sacramento

The most interesting neighborhood places in America's farm-to-fork capital

## SECOND EDITION

## CECILY HASTINGS

A SPECIAL
THANK YOU
TO OUR SPONSORS

Visit Sacramento
East Sacramento Chamber of Commerce
Midtown Association
Rita Gibson Financial Services
Golden Pacific Bank
Elise Brown Realtor
Bardis Homes
Downtown Sacramento Partnership
The Handle District
Oak Park Business Association
City Councilmember Jeff Harris
City Councilmember Steve Hansen
Sacramento State University

INSIDE PUBLICATIONS

This book is dedicated to my mother, Virginia Hayward, who helped publish the first book on her small town's history in 1976. Her love of community and spirit of volunteerism remain with me every day of my life.

Cecily Hastings

## PUBLISHED BY INSIDE PUBLICATIONS

3104 O Street #120
Sacramento, CA 95816
Visit insidesacbook.com

Text and photography copyright © 2018 by Cecily Hastings

All rights reserved.
No part of this book may be used or reproduced in any manner without written permission from the publisher, except in the context of reviews.

Book design by Cecily Hastings, Brian Burch and Daniel Nardinelli

Library of Congress Cataloging-in-Publication data is available upon request.

Every effort was made to ensure the accuracy of the information in this book at press time. However, certain details are subject to change. The publisher cannot accept responsibility for any consequences arising from the use of this book.

Printed and bound in China
978-1-64316-868-5
Second Edition

| | |
|---|---|
| INSIDE  CITY AMENITIES | 8 |
| INSIDE  Downtown | 18 |
| INSIDE  Old Sac & Bridge District | 52 |
| INSIDE  R Street | 62 |
| INSIDE  Midtown & Sutter District | 78 |
| INSIDE  the Handle | 118 |
| INSIDE  Land & Curtis Parks | 130 |
| INSIDE  Oak Park | 150 |
| INSIDE  East Sac | 166 |

# INTRODUCTION

Sacramento is known as America's Farm-to-Fork Capital. No other major American city is more centrally located amid so many small, family-owned farms, ranches and vineyards—all producing year-round in our ideal Mediterranean climate. Sacramento adopted the Farm-to-Fork Capital designation through the efforts of civic and business leaders who wanted to sing the praises of our local food-growing and food-making experience.

Sacramento is also home to one of the largest farmers markets in the state: the famed Sunday farmers market Downtown, an exciting marketplace of fruits, vegetables, meat, fish, flowers and artisanal products. In Sacramento, some 40 other farmers markets attract tens of thousands of people each week seeking the farm-to-fork experience.

Sacramento celebrates farm-to-fork culture each September with a festival and other events capped by a gala dinner at which hundreds of diners enjoy a locally sourced meal on the magnificent Tower Bridge. The original celebrity chef—Jeremiah Tower—recently referred to Sacramento as "the epicenter of food."

Guests are treated to a feast highlighting the delicious collaboration between the Sacramento region's farmers and chefs. The honored chefs selected to create the dinner are given a special green logo on their restaurant's page in this book.

But Sacramento doesn't always get the respect it deserves. Even though it is the state capital, it's often overshadowed by its larger and louder regional neighbors.

The discovery of gold in the Sacramento Valley in early 1848 sparked the historic Gold Rush. But in recent years, another rush has occurred: the development of the city's many diverse neighborhoods. People are attracted to these neighborhoods by the sheer number of interesting shops, restaurants, cafés and other commercial establishments. In addition, the new Golden 1 Center Downtown has encouraged dozens of new developments that enrich the central city and beyond, bringing people from all over to dine, shop, explore and be entertained.

This book is a curated collection of Sacramento's most interesting places, along with our city's most creative arts and cultural experiences. It's designed to give readers an insider's glimpse into our unique and exceptional Sacramento neighborhoods. It's not meant just for people who live in Sacramento, but also for visitors from all over the world who come on business or vacation or are considering moving here. The eight neighborhoods profiled in this book are among the city's most pleasant to visit on foot and by bike.

Sacramento is perfect for raising families, so we have indicated the places that especially welcome them.

This book was lovingly crafted as a guide to the delightful locally owned places we know about from living here and publishing neighborhood newsmagazines for the past two decades. Find yourself in Sacramento!

—Cecily Hastings

# ART GALLERIES

Insiders know Sacramento is more than a company town for political science—it's also an artists' colony. A deeply rooted tradition of celebrating and supporting local artists can be found across the city, highlighted in September when Verge Center for the Arts presents Sac Open Studios, an annual monthlong arts party. Sac Open showcases more than 150 emerging and established artists. In spring, summer and fall, Second Saturdays become an organic, eclectic expression of the arts and include culinary, visual and performing events.

Here is a glimpse of the work of a few of Sacramento's most established gallery artists. Top left to right: Jeff Myers, Elisabeth Higgins O'Conner and Tim Collom. Middle left to right: Kathrine Lemke Waste and Matt Bult. Bottom left to right: Elaine Bowers, Julia Couzens and Bryan Valenzuela. Some of the city's most interesting galleries and studios include:

**ARTHOUSE on R**
1021 R Street
arthouseonr.com

**ArtSpace1616**
1616 Del Paso Boulevard

**Archival Gallery**
3223 Folsom Boulevard
archivalgallery.com

**Beatnik Studios**
723 S Street
beatnik-studios.com

**b. sakato garo**
923 20th Street
bsakatagaro.com

**CK Art Gallery**
2500 J Street
ckart-gallery.com

**Elliott Fouts Gallery**
1831 P Street
efgallery.com

**JayJay**
5524 B Elvas Avenue
jayjayart.com

**Patris Studio and Art Gallery**
3460 2nd Avenue
patrisstudiogallery.blogspot.com

**Sparrow Gallery**
1021 R Street
sparrowgallerysacramento.com

**Tim Collom Gallery**
915 20th Street
timcollomgallery.com

**The Brickhouse Gallery & Art Complex**
2837 36th Street
thebrickhouseartgallery.com

**The Gregory Kondos Gallery**
Fischbacher Fine Arts Building
Sacramento City College

**The Robert Else Gallery and The University Library Gallery**
Kadema Hall
Sacramento State University

**Verge Center for the Arts**
625 S Street
vergeart.com

# LADY BIRD: THE MOVIE

Sacramento takes a star turn in "Lady Bird," the sweet coming-of-age movie about a young woman full of dreams in the capital city. "Lady Bird" earned five Academy Award nominations, including Best Picture and Best Director for Greta Gerwig, the River Park native who based the screenplay loosely on her own experiences at St. Francis High School. Gerwig lives in New York these days, but plans several more films with a Sacramento backdrop. Meantime, local movie fans can walk (or run) past locations that became part of the "Lady Bird" narrative. Sacramento Running Tours has arranged courses that trek past various sites with cameo appearances in the movie, including the McKinley Rose Garden and East Sac's Club Raven, which has created a drink to honor the city's favorite bird. Artist Maren Conrad's mural in Midtown at 901 16th Street celebrates Gerwig's contribution to the city. The original copy of the movie's script—signed by Gerwig—was recently gifted by local businesswoman and philanthropist Rita Gibson to the Special Collections of the Sacramento Public Library.

# PERFORMING ARTS

Live theater and musical performances are treasured in Sacramento and they abound throughout the city. B Street Theatre is renowned for innovative productions of new plays and performances designed for children. The company has a stunning new home, The Sofia at 27th and Capitol. The city's oldest troupe is the Sacramento Theatre Company, whose complex at 14th and H streets brings vitality to traditional and contemporary works. The Sacramento Ballet is the city's premier dance company, and the Sacramento Philharmonic and Opera inspires classical aficionados. Song and dance fans cheer Broadway Sacramento for keeping the show on the road with the Broadway on Tour and Broadway at Music Circus, Sacramento's favorite summertime theater-in-the-round performance series. Smaller arts companies include Capital Stage and Ovation Stage that entertain with intimate and provocative productions in Midtown. Sacramento Choral Society and Orchestra is an auditioned, volunteer chorus with a professional orchestra. Celebration Arts creates African-American performing arts experiences with plays, training and special events. Capital Dance Project is an independent collective of professional dancers. Sacramento365.com is the place to find almost every performance being held in the region.

**sacramento365.com**

**B Street Theatre**
bstreettheatre.org

**Sacramento Choral Society and Orchestra**
sacramentochoral.com

**Sacramento Theatre Company**
sactheatre.org

**Sacramento Ballet**
sacballet.org

**Sacramento Philharmonic and Opera**
sacphilopera.org

**Sacramento Youth Symphony**
sacramentoyouthsymphony.org

**Sacramento Children's Chorus**
sacramentochildrenschorus.org

**Broadway Sacramento Music Circus**
broadwaysacramento.com

**Celebration Arts**
celebrationarts.net

**Capital Dance Project**
capitaldanceproject.org

**Capital Stage**
capstage.org

**Big Idea Theater**
bigideatheatre.org

**Ovation Stage**
ovationstage.com

**Vox Musica**
voxmusica.net

# CITY OF MURALS

They surround us, brightening our lives and lending color and vibrancy to the cityscape's brick and mortar canvas. Over the past four decades, Sacramento artists have produced more than 600 murals on walls around the city. Now the art form has blossomed into a summer festival—Wide Open Walls. For 10 days, more than 40 artists create dozens of murals to celebrate the relevancy and diversity of street art. Wide Open Walls includes gallery openings, mural tours, artist receptions, panel discussions, First Friday and Second Saturday celebrations and opportunities to watch murals being created. The festival offers a mural-finding map on its website at wow916.com.

Artist Credits: Top left clockwise: Jose Di Gregorio, Tavar Zawacki and Jorit Agoch, Andrew Schoultz, S.V. Williams and Molly Devlin, Bryan Valenzuela, Micah Crandall-Bear and Adnate. Center left to right: a mural by Ludo and Bryan Valenzuela at work.

**Wide Open Walls**
**wow916.com**

Dr. Ernie Bodai

# SACRAMENTO WALK OF STARS

Incredible accomplishments by Sacramento's best are now indelible. The Sacramento Walk of Stars brightens the cityscape with bronze and terrazzo stars in the Handle District on L Street between 18th and 19th streets. The Walk of Stars made its debut in 2016 and honored Olympic swimmer and three-time gold medalist Debbie Meyer, world-renowned artist Gregory Kondos, groundbreaking breast cancer surgeon Dr. Ernie Bodai, celebrated actor and director LeVar Burton and rock legend Timothy B. Schmit of the Eagles. The 2017 honorees included acclaimed author Nicholas Sparks, iconic founder of Tower Records Russ Solomon, Olympian and humanitarian Billy Mills and U.S. Olympic basketball and WNBA star Ruthie Bolton. In Sacramento's newest tradition, honorees gather to have their stars unveiled and proceed to a gala dinner at Memorial Auditorium. At dinner, the stars share stories of success and describe how the community inspired them on their journey to national and global achievement.

sacramentowalkofstars.com

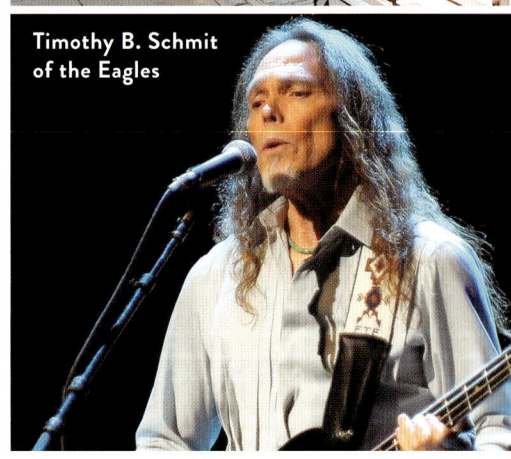

Timothy B. Schmit of the Eagles

Olympian Debbie Meyer

Olympian Ruthie Bolton

"Sacramento River with Boat" by Artist Gregory Kondos

Actor and Activist LeVar Burton

Author and Philanthropist Nicholas Sparks

Olympian Billy Mills

# INSIDE Downtown

Downtown Commons – DOCO – is the latest addition to Sacramento's always-evolving central core. Along with its Jeff Koons "Coloring Book" sculpture, DOCO is anchored by Golden 1 Center and the Kimpton Sawyer Hotel, and surrounded by a host of new shops, restaurants and bars.

While DOCO represents the contemporary, adjacent downtown streets reflect Sacramento's heritage with the Capitol Building, Capitol Park and the International World Peace Rose Garden, the reimagined Sacramento Valley Station, Memorial Auditorium and dozens of places to dine out and enjoy a craft beer, regional wine or bespoke cocktail.

The Crocker Art Museum houses some of the West's finest historic and modern art works, plus exhibits featuring internationally renowned artists. Enjoy Sacramento's famed farm-to-fork culture direct from the source every Sunday at the Southside Park farmer's market.

INSIDE *Downtown*

## ANDY'S CANDY APOTHECARY

Glass jars sparkle with sweet treats along the shelves of Andy's Candy Apothecary, a nostalgic downtown wonderland for every candy aficionado. Open since 2013, the sweet shop is a magical place realized by owner Andy Paul, whose victory in Sacramento's first-ever Calling All Dreamers contest provided support to open the Apothecary. Paul won business services, rent and construction expenses. He transformed the opportunity into the candy store of his dreams. Today, Paul is Sacramento's resident candy expert. He's delighted to unravel the mysteries of sweets and can explain why all candy bars are not created equal, or how some Swedish fish are better than others. As a youngster, Paul spent allowance money and cash from his newspaper route on penny sweets and drugstore candy bars. These days, his business provides the world's finest sugary confections to customers of all ages.

**1012 9th Street**
**916.905.4115**
andyscandystore.com

INSIDE *Downtown*

# CROCKER ART MUSEUM

California art, works on paper, European art, international ceramics, photography, Asian art, African and Oceanic art and more—such is the diverse beauty awaiting discovery at the Crocker Art Museum. As the oldest public art museum in the West, the Crocker fulfills its cultural mission with expansive galleries and educational facilities that delight all ages. Built as a family mansion in 1885 by Edwin B. Crocker, the museum elevated its status as a regional destination in 2010 with the new Teel Family Pavilion. Ten years in the creation, the Pavilion adds 125,000 square feet to Crocker's historic mansion. The expansion more than tripled the museum's size and gave the Crocker dedicated gallery spaces for all collecting areas. The historic wing's first floor serves as the Education Center, which includes four studio classrooms, space for student and community exhibits, the expanded Gerald Hansen Library, the Art Education Resource Room and Tot Land. Traveling exhibitions—Andy Warhol, Edward Hopper and Norman Rockwell were favorites—join the Crocker's beautiful collections. And the Crocker's Museum Store is the downtown destination for stylish, artistically inspired gifts and one-of-a-kind designs. Purchases support the museum's exhibits and programs. The Crocker Café serves snacks all day and offers counter service at lunch. Museum admission is not required to enjoy the café, elegant lobby, patio setting and store.

**216 O Street**
**916.808.7000**
**crockerart.org**

# ALLSPICERY

A world of spice can be found in one location at Sacramento's ultimate culinary specialty shop. Allspicery is exactly what the name suggests—a place where the world's most difficult-to-find spices present themselves for adventurous chefs, both home-style and professional. The winner of the 2015 Downtown Sacramento Foundation's third annual Calling All Dreamers competition—where local hopefuls submit business plans to be considered for monetary awards that help make their retail dreams a reality—Allspicery is the vision of Heather Wong. A culinary enthusiast who had become frustrated with the scarcity of ethnic spices in Sacramento, Wong decided to take matters into her own hands and make global spices available to the community. An avid traveler, Wong was determined to deliver the flavors of the world to her adopted hometown. In the quaint Allspicery shop, chefs can experiment from among about 300 spices, most of which have been impossible to obtain at traditional retail outlets in Sacramento. Clients can purchase spices whole or have them freshly ground by Wong in-house to flavor special or daily dishes.

**1125 11th Street**
**916.389.7828**
**allspicery.com**

INSIDE *Downtown*

## ESQUIRE GRILL

Elegant décor, soft lighting, rich mahogany wood floors and walls, and high-backed banquettes of tufted black leather make the Esquire Grill the perfect setting for political power lunches and dinner before the theater. Located at the bustling corner of 13th and K Streets, the Esquire Grill is surrounded by the Sacramento Convention Center, Community Center Theater, Esquire IMAX theater and the Hyatt Regency and Sheraton Grand hotels. With the State Capitol two blocks away, Esquire Grill serves as the town's top spot for celebrity sightings. Arnold Schwarzenegger was a regular as governor and a constellation of stars from Clint Eastwood to Gwyneth Paltrow have dropped by for lunch. The seasonal menu showcases classic dishes like the Dungeness crab and shrimp Louie salad. The ahi tuna burger is a favorite among legislators and lobbyists, served with spicy soy mayonnaise, pickled ginger, red onion and daikon sprouts. Grilled New York steak or a half-pound Angus burger will tempt heartier diners. Esquire Grill has a full bar and an extensive California wine list. Another fine touch from this restaurant is a well-seasoned wait staff, sure to please.

**1213 K Street**
**916.448.8900**
**paragarys.com**

INSIDE *Downtown*

## GRANGE RESTAURANT & BAR

Celebrating the flavors and freshness of Central Valley fruits and vegetables, Grange is where locals and travelers alike savor California's finest sustainable cuisine. Located at The Citizen Hotel at 10th and J streets, Grange serves as a food ambassador, sourcing its menu from regional farms that include Capay Organic, Del Rio Botanical and Soil Born Farms. The menu celebrates the bounty of the region, and combined with international and regional influences makes this a quintessential farm-to-fork dining destination. Artisanal cooking can be enjoyed in the Private Dining Room, where parties of up to 20 are served on the mezzanine level overlooking the main dining room. The Chef's Table allows for a family-style tasting menu.

926 J Street
916.492.4450
grangesacramento.com

INSIDE *Downtown*

## CAFETERIA 15L

Reminiscent of the classic American lunch counter spiced with a millennial flavor, Cafeteria 15L serves an eclectic array of comfort food that foodies appreciate. Lunch favorites include elevated delicacies such as truffle tater tots, French fries served in faux newsprint, macaroni and cheese, Caesar salad, meatloaf and the enduringly popular French dip sandwich, tossed back with a glass of plantation iced tea or house-made fruit punch. Dinner resolves any cravings for buttermilk fried chicken strips or onion strings, chicken and waffles or braised beef short ribs served with mushroom risotto. And there's brunch, where chocolate banana waffles, brioche French toast, inventive skillets and benedicts indulge all appetites. Designed by the interior artists who brought the look of the W Hotels chain to the world, Cafeteria 15L features two plush outdoor patios, a comfortable lounge space and large areas dedicated to private and semi-private dining, plus the main dining room. Reclaimed woods, industrial light fixtures and an array of mixed and matched chairs create an atmosphere whimsical and cozy. The familiar cafeteria has never looked cooler—another success story from the local Wong family of restaurants, led by brothers Mason, Curtis and Alan Wong.

**1116 15th Street**
**916.492.1960**
*cafeteria15l.com*

# DOWNTOWN & VINE

Expanding the Sacramento community's exposure to unique wines from California and around the globe is the mission of Downtown & Vine. With two wine clubs for customers and servings offered in tasting flights, glasses or by the bottle, Downtown & Vine provides the opportunity and atmosphere to taste and compare the region's best wines, craft beers and international labels. The Downtown K Street location, just a block from the Community Center Theater, provides an inviting atmosphere for after-work gatherings. The kitchen creates masterful small plates—tapas, flatbreads and charcuterie—to enhance the vibe. Downtown & Vine's retail selection is maintained by a knowledgeable staff and carries a vast selection of wine and beer to take home or send as gifts. The store can ship to 42 states, making long-distance gift shopping simple.

**1200 K Street**
**916.228.4518**
**downtownandvine.com**

## CHOCOLATE FISH COFFEE ROASTERS

Life at Chocolate Fish Downtown revolves around the heavenly complexities of small-batch coffee. Like its sister operation in East Sacramento, this coffee bar takes its business seriously and treats the humble bean with reverence. Every sip reflects a taste conjured from beans harvested within the past year. Proprietors Andy and Edie Baker ensure those beans are the finest available, whether from Central or South America or Africa. The sleek shop at Third and Q streets features a polished concrete floor and accents of teal and chrome. The location makes Chocolate Fish's unique coffee convenient to people who work at the state office campus south of Capitol Mall or CalPERS headquarters, right across the street. Chocolate Fish merchandise shares shelf space with bags of fresh-roasted coffee to take home.

**400 P Street**
**916.400.4204**
chocolatefishcoffee.com
**Opening 2018**
**2940 Freeport Boulevard**
**Land Park**

INSIDE *Downtown*

## DE VERE'S IRISH PUB

A corner of Ireland's capital has been transported 6,000 miles to create this lively downtown pub. The de Vere White family comes from a long line of pub owners who emigrated from Dublin to the U.S. After settling in Sacramento, the family decided to re-establish their hometown experience, including 20-ounce pints of beer and lovingly poured Guinness Stout. The family contracted with Irish craftsmen to design and build each of the pub's fixtures and furnishings. The pieces were shipped from Ireland and reassembled in Sacramento. Personal touches, including photos, paintings and antiques from the de Vere White home in Ireland, were added to complete the masterpiece. European and American sports are always on the big screens. Brothers Henry (seated) and Simon de Vere White (standing, third from left) are shown here along with executive chef Wes Nilssen and managing partner Josey McCarter. The food is classically Irish, including sliders, sandwiches, Granny's shepherd's pie, bangers and mash, and a fry-up made with bacon brined in-house. Over two dozen Irish whiskeys are featured, including at least six types of Jameson.

1521 L Street
916.231.9947
deverespub.com

Inside *Downtown*

## ELLA DINING ROOM & BAR

A Downtown Sacramento institution and premier dining destination, Ella Dining Room & Bar serves New American, farm-to-fork cuisine for lunch, dinner and happy hour, featuring entrées of seafood, steaks and pastas, small plates, salads, fresh oysters and traditional caviar service. Ella also features an award-winning wine list as well as seasonal and classic hand-crafted cocktails at its renowned bar. Acclaimed for food, service, design and ambiance, Ella has also earned numerous local awards and honors. Ella Dining Room & Bar is family owned and operated by Selland Family Restaurants co-founders, husband-and-wife chefs Randall Selland and Nancy Zimmer and their grown children, Josh Nelson and Tamera Baker. For 27 years, the Selland family has been committed to promoting local and sustainable growers, farmers and ranchers, and to creating fresh, honest and innovative dishes featuring the highest quality seasonal and regionally sourced ingredients at Ella and its sister restaurants, The Kitchen, Selland's Market-Café and OBO' Italian Table and Bar.

**1131 K Street (at 12th Street)**
**916.443.3772**
**elladiningroomandbar.com**

Inside *Downtown*

# FIRESTONE PUBLIC HOUSE

Sports and happy hours have never looked, sounded and tasted so good in Sacramento as they do at Firestone Public House. This is a serious place for people in unserious moods—whether looking to unwind after work or catch a ballgame with friends. The beer menu is comprehensive and exhaustive, with 60 handles on tap. The televised sports options span the globe, from baseball and football to soccer and even cricket, depending on what's happening wherever, delivered on 22 flat-screen monitors with an unrivaled sound system. Two outdoor patios bring the party under the sun, moon and stars. Menus are classically American and locally inspired. They feature multicultural options as imagined by the owners, the Wong brothers—Mason, Curtis and Alan. Among the most popular dishes are delectable finger foods such as chicken wings, avocado eggrolls, banh mi sliders and pulled pork nachos. Firestone features salads, soups, epic pizzas (including one for breakfast), mouthwatering sandwiches, including Sriracha-candied bacon grilled cheese, and entrees such as beef potpie, baby back ribs and beer-battered fish and chips.

1132 16th Street
916.446.0888
firestonepublichouse.com

INSIDE *Downtown*

# FRANK FAT'S

This venerable Chinese food restaurant in the heart of downtown is a true testament to the American dream. The founder of the eponymous eatery immigrated to America from China in 1919 at age 16 with no money or identification and managed to open one of the city's most iconic restaurants a mere 20 years later. Frank Fat's is now the anchor restaurant of the four establishments in the Fat Family Restaurant Group. It continues to impress with its fine dining menu and elegant interior 80 years later under the watchful eye of Fat's youngest son, Jerry. Traditional favorites include house made pot stickers, Mandarin duck, Szechuan beef, honey walnut prawns that melt in your mouth and amazing assortments of chow mein, chow fun and fried rice, along with Fat's specialty dishes like wok-fried spare ribs, brandy-fried chicken, a special-recipe wor won ton soup and their most decadent offering, a 16-ounce New York steak smothered in onions and oyster sauce. Leave room for dessert and treat yourself to the best banana cream pie in town. With dishes this iconic and an atmosphere this cool—check out the rosy-lit full bar—it's not hard to see why Fat's has drawn crowds for nearly a century.

**806 L Street**
**916.442.7092**
**frankfats.com**

INSIDE *Downtown*

## MA JONG'S ASIAN DINER

Never mind the ancient game played with plastic tiles. At this Downtown restaurant, the name Ma Jong pays tribute to the matriarchs of a centuries-old family dynasty and combines the culinary cultures of Japan, Thailand, Vietnam and China. The unique flavors from those countries reveal their profiles in each of Ma Jong's dishes. Aromas mingle and create an atmosphere at once homey and exotic. Daily specials feature meats, fresh fish and crisp vegetables, simmering in soy, teriyaki, basil and peanut sauces. The interior of Ma Jong's Asian Diner is meant to evoke images of a village, with natural wood countertops, low-back seats and several communal tables. Dangling lanterns cast a soft glow on the exposed ductwork and brick walls to remind customers they are in the heart of the city enjoying adventurous Asian fare. Watching over the experience is a 300-year-old Buddha. Downtown workers bundle off takeaway boxes of Shanghai spicy chow mein. Central city residents call orders in and await the arrival of the delivery rickshaw emblazoned with Ma Jong's enigmatic face. The restaurant is a convenient stop for theatergoers eager for a quick bite before curtain time at the Community Center Theater one block east.

**1431 L Street**
**916.442.7555**
majongs.com

# SOUTH

On a quiet stretch of 11th Street in the Southside Park neighborhood, a little bistro combines two modern trends in neighborhood dining: unaffected casualness and back-to-basics cooking. The owners are N'Gina and Ian Kavookjian, and they base their menu and restaurant's philosophy on timeless traditions of Southern cooking. Or, as the owners describe it, "At South, we are not trying to reinvent the wheel, we are just trying to express 200 years of our family's story on a 12-inch plate." The family history is a gorgeous mix of traditional Southern and Cajun cooking styles. Yams, fried green tomatoes and hushpuppies are all on point. The standout dish is the fried chicken, a classic take on a familiar meal that becomes something remarkable at South. People talk of South's fried chicken in hushed voices and reverent tones, and many knowing fans believe there is no better example of this Southern kitchen essential, at least not west of the Mississippi. Order at the counter and then select your table inside or on the charming patio for service.

**2005 11th Street**
**916.382.9722**
**weheartfriedchicken.com**

# SOLOMON'S DELICATESSEN

A Jewish deli with a legendary legacy–that's Solomon's Delicatessen, named for Tower Records founder and Sacramento icon Russ Solomon, who died in March 2018 at age 92. Co-owner Andrea Lepore defines the food as "Newish Jewish," but Solomon's delivers a classic bounty of timeless deli feasts that include pastrami sandwiches and smoked fish. There's a contemporary side to Solomon's, with farm-to-fork touches such as homemade schmear, all from the skilled hands of chef Aimal Formoli. In recognition of the deli's namesake, Lepore tracked down historic photos of Solomon and his culture-bending empire. The restaurant features a slick interior mix of marble, wood and leather accents to complement the vibrant 1970s-era mural by graphic designer Frank Carson out front. The location on K Street near Seventh is fitting: it was a Tower store from 1973 to 2006.

**730 K Street**
solomonsdelicatessen.com

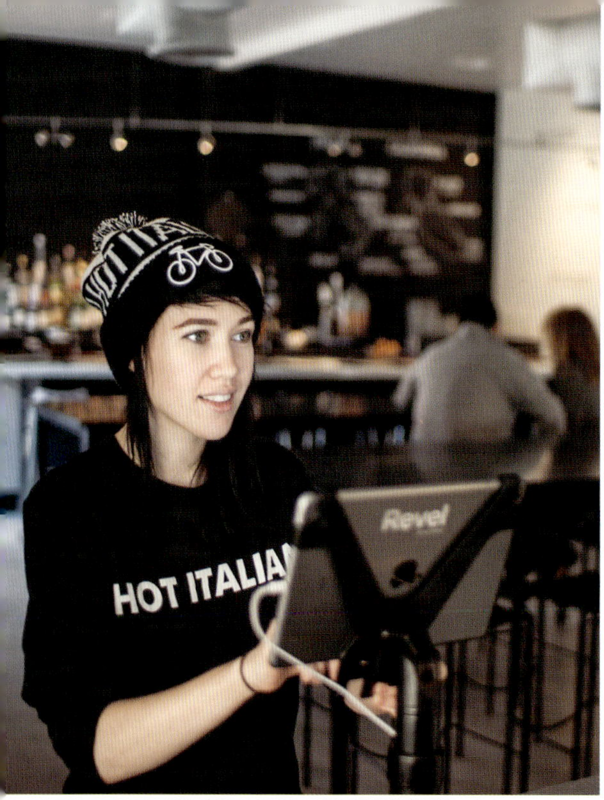
Revel
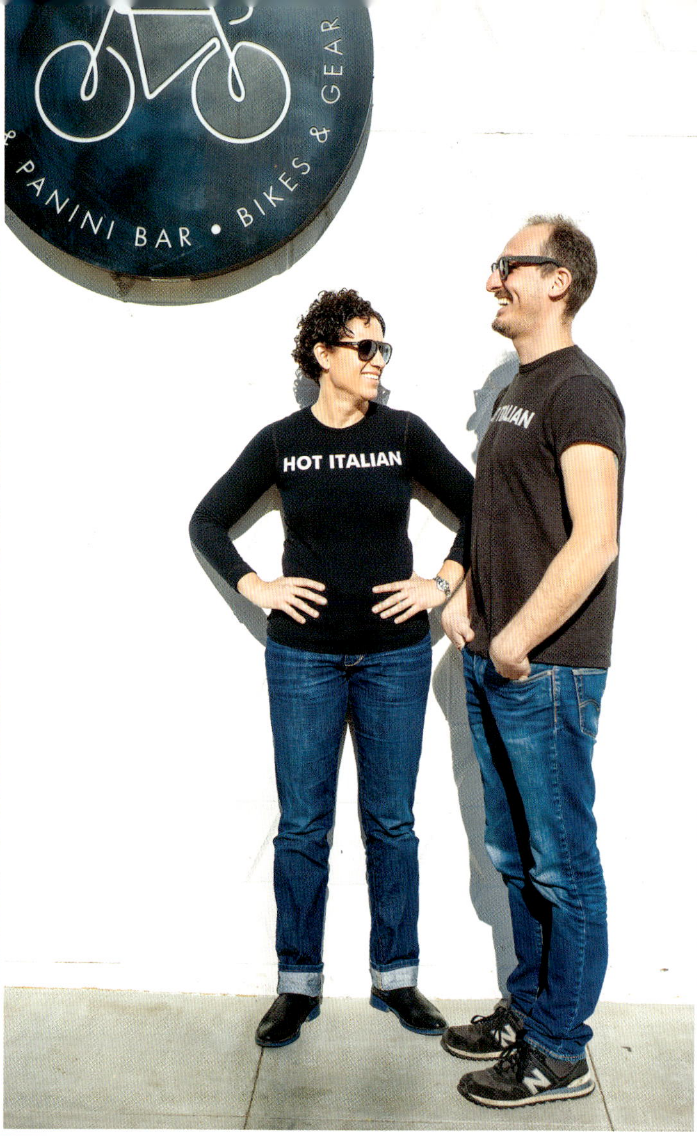
& PANINI BAR • BIKES & GEAR
HOT ITALIAN
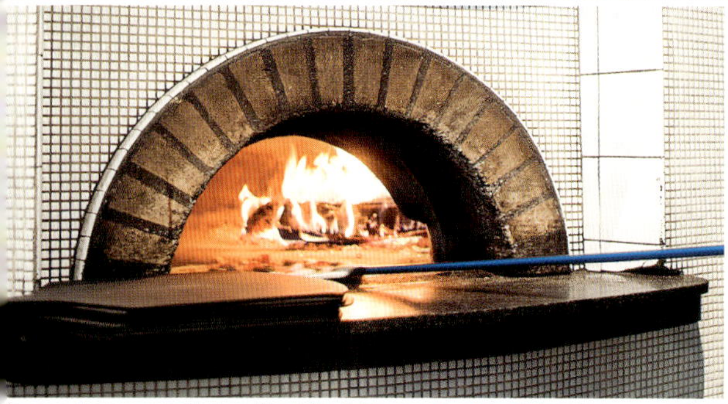
HOTITALIAN
HOTITALIAN

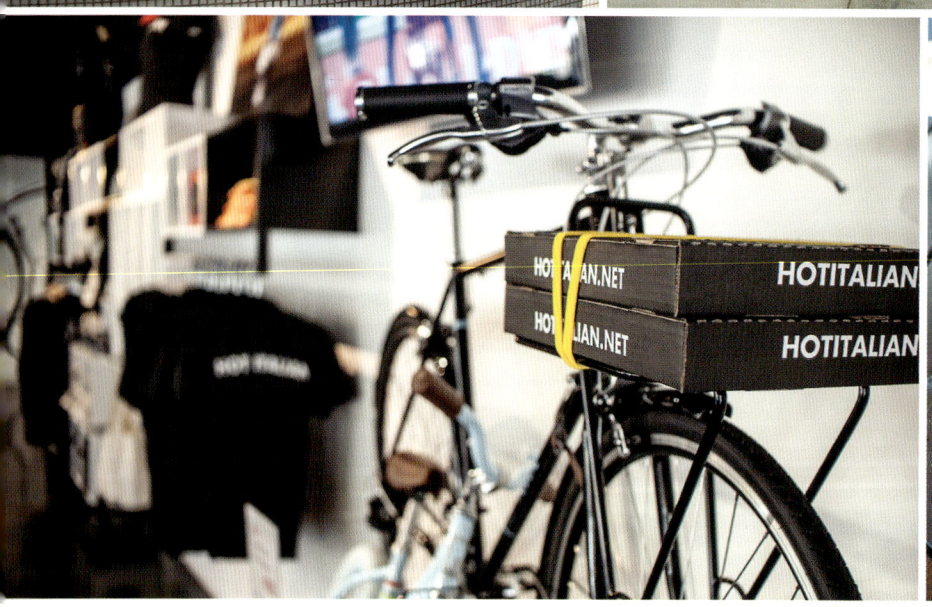

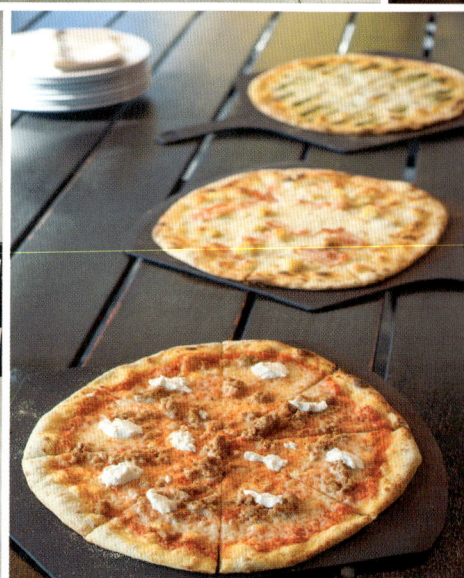

INSIDE *Downtown*

# HOT ITALIAN

Their mission was to build a place where delicious pizza brings people together. Their motto became *tutto e possibile*—anything is possible. The formula worked. Anything is possible at Hot Italian. Consider the Bortolami, a celebration of house-made fennel sausage, seasonal mushrooms, tomato sauce, smoked mozzarella and treviso radicchio. Or the Fiori, which combines prosciutto parma, mozzarella, mushrooms, tomato sauce, arugula and Bariani truffle oil. Beyond its remarkably inventive pizza, Hot Italian celebrates a joy for life. The restaurant is filled with friends eager to celebrate spontaneity in art, music, design and sports. The owners are Andrea Lepore, an Italian-American from a family of artists, and Fabrizio Cercatore, an artistic *pizzaiolo*, or master pizza maker, from the Italian Riviera region of Cinque Terre. They built a European-style community gathering place, where soccer matches and cycling events play on monitors and Vespa scooters supplement the space. Gelato in flavors like caramel salato, chocolate orange, limon, peanut butter chip, stracciatella and white mint chip complete the magic.

**1627 16th Street**
**916.444.3000**
**hotitalian.net**

# PRESERVATION & CO.

In the hands of Jason Poole (shown) and Brad Peters, pickled habanero pepper chips become a work of gastronomical art. Poole and Peters are business partners and brining experts who preserve delicious and healthy produce from local farms without artificial colors, flavors or preservatives. They capture zesty flavors that make tongues dance. The team behind the "Sacramento born and brined" brand specializes in hand-packed products created in their compact location behind a roll-up door along an industrial stretch of 19th Street. From this hideaway, they sell to more than 400 retail locations across the country. Preservation & Co. features an inventory that includes cocktail mixes—Bloody Mary mix, blackberry and jalapeño margarita—and pickles, sriracha sauces, citrus rosemary salt and ghost pepper salt, plus bar and pantry supplies and clothing. The pickles alone are amazing, from balsamic beet slices, habanero chips, jalapeño onion strips and cayenne carrot sticks, to hefeweizen bread and butter chips, hickory Brussels sprouts, horseradish green beans and black pepper asparagus. The outpost of Preservation & Co. is a gathering place for flavor aficionados, who appreciate the shop's liberal sampling policy.

**1717 19th Street**
**916.706.1044**
**preservationandco.com**

# TIME TESTED BOOKS

Behind a brick façade on 21st Street, inside a 19th-century building, Time Tested Books is a portal to another time and place. Since 1981, owner Peter Keat has made it his mission to stock his cozy bookshop with an impressive array of new and used titles, including rare and out-of-print books and vinyl records. Keat and his knowledgeable staff assist guests in search of specific and difficult-to-find titles. And for clients hoping to reduce their own collections, Time Tested Books buys and trades books and records. The shop serves as host to a variety of events such as author signings, readings, lectures and musical performances, all certain to inspire and enlighten the book lover and culture devotee in all of us. Be sure to say hello to Keat's adorable dog, Marco, when making a visit.

**1114 21st Street**
**916.447.5696**
**timetestedbooks.blogspot.com**

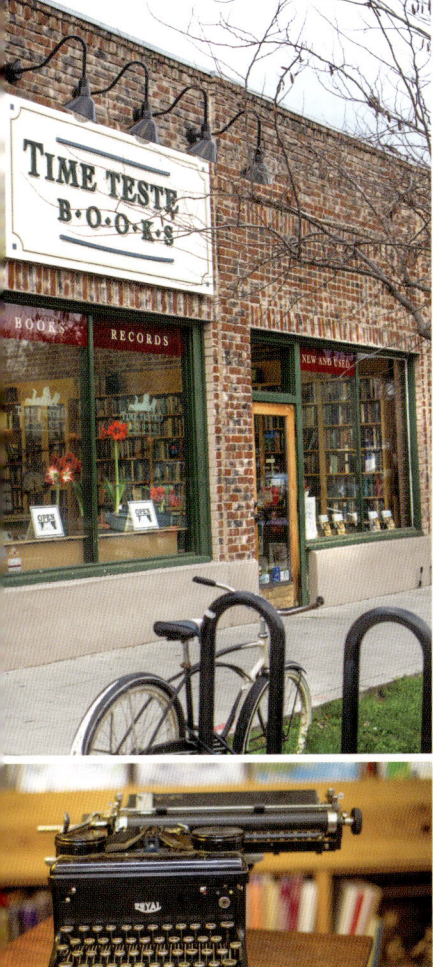
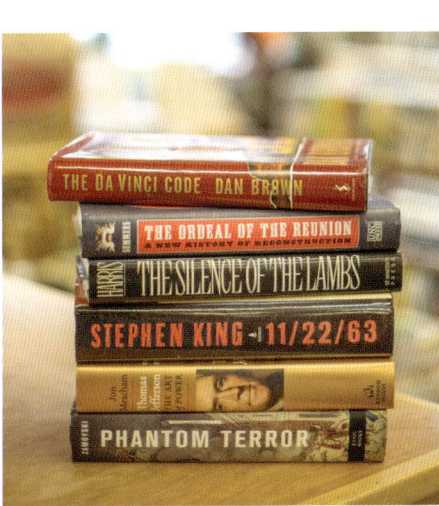

# MAYAHUEL

"An experience for the senses" is a promise fulfilled at Tequila Museo Mayahuel, commonly referred to as Mayahuel. This inspiring place succeeds with an impressive environment of colorful sculptures and murals, authentic home-cooked recipes and astonishing selections of tequila. The bar and restaurant blend together seamlessly at Mayahuel, which was named after Maya, the daughter of owner Ernesto Delgado. Cultural influences from Mexico appear with a series of rotating art exhibits, mariachi bands and regional food specialties. The home cooking of Delgado's mother inspires much of the menu. As for the drinks, guests should prepare for an education in the art of tequila. Small batch, artisanal and popular brands are served, along with original cocktails based on tequila. Adventurous agave fans will find a plentiful supply of mescal.

1200 K Street
916.441.7200
experiencemayahuel.com

# LA COSECHA

If Downtown Sacramento has a geographic heart, it would be Cesar Chavez Plaza, located across from the city's historic city hall and site of a weekly farmers market. La Cosecha is a festive and welcoming place to linger, eat and drink indoors or outdoors on the plaza. The walk-up taco bar, operated by Ernesto Delgado—who also runs Mayahuel on K Street and Mesa Mercado in Carmichael—features a deep selection of tacos and more. Lunch and dinner menus include stew, chile verde, carnitas, enchiladas, salads, tortas and a specialty hamburger. A favorite is the CDMX Street Fries—tossed in cascabel chili salt and topped with house-made chorizo, fundido cheese and poblano crema. La Cosecha serves colorful cocktails plus six handles of draft beer and cider. Or there's always Corona by the bucket.

**917 9th Street in Cesar Chavez Plaza**
**916.970.5354**
lacosechasacramento.com

# INSIDE *Old Sac*

Tourists love the place, but there's plenty for locals as well in Old Sacramento. The National Historic Landmark and State Historic Park features 296 acres filled with the West's largest collection of significant buildings, each of them relevant to the Gold Rush and California history. Most of the restored buildings house restaurants, bars, shops and museums.

Weekend street festivals are frequent on the cobblestone streets, and the Sacramento River Train runs southbound excursions from the Central Pacific Freight Depot, a few steps down Front Street from the internationally famed California State Railroad Museum.

# INSIDE *Bridge District*

With the Tower Bridge as its golden gateway, the Bridge District is West Sacramento's new connection to the action in Old Sacramento and Downtown Commons. The Bridge District creates its own momentum, with river walks, Raley Field – home of the Sacramento River Cats baseball team – and the Barn, a creative outdoor stage, beer garden and restaurant. The district also features one of the region's most exciting collections of contemporary riverfront residences.

INSIDE *Bridge District*

## THE BARN

It's not really a barn. No, the Barn is a soaring land bridge that highlights an eclectic public space in the booming Bridge District of West Sacramento. There's an entertainment element with outdoor performances scheduled every Saturday night from May through September. In time for Summer 2018, there will be a beer garden operated by Drake's Brewing Company, an East Bay favorite with locations in San Leandro and Oakland. The Barn was developed by Fulcrum Property and stands adjacent to the Sacramento River. With its shingled exterior and organic aura, the Barn pays respect to the community's rural roots. The structure's gently curved design is by !melk, a New York firm famed for inventing creative public spaces in Las Vegas, Miami and Phoenix, among other places.

**985 Riverfront Street**
**West Sacramento**
**916.383.3333**
**barn.thebridgedistrict.com**

INSIDE *Old Sac*

## RIO CITY CAFÉ

Husband-and-wife owners Mark and Stephanie Miller opened Rio City Café in 1994 in a stylishly rustic building designed to resemble a steamship warehouse from the late 1800s. The concept was perfect. The restaurant blends seamlessly with the quaint, historic charms of the Old Sacramento riverfront. The casual setting, overseen by general manager Scott Meier (shown seated), features indoor and outdoor seating, room for banquets, and Tower Bridge and riverfront views that match the inspiration of a fresh, farm-to-fork menu. While Rio City dishes are distinctively Californian, executive chef Lai Saepharn combines local, house-made ingredients—favorites include ahi nachos, jambalaya, specialty meats and seafood—and can accommodate any diet. A full bar includes craft beers, specialty cocktails and a wine list of Napa and local labels.

1110 Front Street
916.442.8226
riocitycafe.com

INSIDE *Old Sac*

## THE FIREHOUSE RESTAURANT

Smoked tenderloin carpaccio. Lobster bisque. Filet mignon. Veal porterhouse. Famed for perennial excellence, The Firehouse Restaurant has been a not-to-be-missed destination for more than 55 years. Housed in a building from 1853 that served as home for the Sacramento No. 3 Fire Brigade, the elegant dining spot was one of Ronald Reagan's favorite places in Sacramento during his eight years as governor—and it's easy to see why. In addition to its rich history, evidenced by it stunning façade and low-lit, grand interior, The Firehouse offers a menu of gourmet classics, matched by a legendary wine list with more than 2,100 labels. Visit the wine cellar to view more than 16,000 bottles housed in the cool depths. Let general manager, wine director and sommelier Mario Ortiz—a Firehouse fixture for more than 40 years—introduce the Vault, a magnificent collection of very rare Californian and European wines. It's no wonder The Firehouse has played host to a star-studded guest list over the years, including Clint Eastwood, Muhammad Ali, Andy Warhol, George Foreman, Michael Jordan and every California governor since the last one to become president.

1112 2nd Street
916.442.4772
firehouseoldsac.com

INSIDE *Old Sac*

# ARTISTS' COLLABORATIVE GALLERY

As the oldest artistic cooperative in Sacramento, the Artists' Collaborative Gallery is precisely what the title suggests: a gathering place for nearly 40 local artists to display and sell beautiful wares. Fine art and ceramics, glass, gourds, jewelry, metal, photography, textiles, wire sculpture, wood and fiber art are available. The member artists, who are invited into the collective studio and store by the collegial membership, are award-winning creators. They come from a wide variety of backgrounds. Inspiring artwork stands out against the dark wood floors and white walls of the converted historical Old Sacramento storefront. Visitors gain a sense of having stepped into a wonderful world of whimsy and creativity. Guests are certain to meet at least one of the artists whose work is on display—the creative talents take turns working in the store. They greet guests and answer questions about the artwork and make the experience truly collaborative.

129 K Street
916.444.7125
artcollab.com

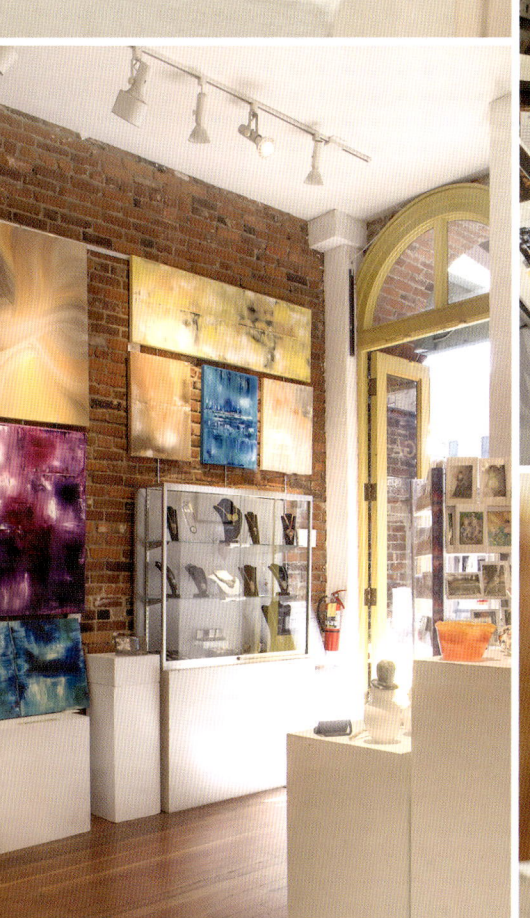

# INSIDE R Street

R Street Corridor was once a thriving warehouse district but now is being transformed into a vibrant new city neighborhood.

R Street is home to locally owned cafes, shops, services and entertainment venues.

WAL (Warehouse Artist Lofts) is a mixed-income community for artists, with four stories of apartments and ground-floor shops and restaurants.

WAL is a place for creative individuals and households to live, work, learn and collaborate with one another.

This is called the Creative Corridor because the corridor's industrial roots have provided a gritty and open canvas for Sacramento's many artists, artisans and entrepreneurs.

INSIDE R Street

# BENJAMINS SHOES

Clearly a man devoted to well-tailored classics, Benjamin Schwartz discovered an old textbook on shoemaking about six years ago and dived headlong into the bespoke shoe crafting business. Today, he runs his unique shop at the back of the Public Market in the bottom floor of the Warehouse Artist Lofts. Benjamins Shoes is the only handmade artisanal shoe shop in Sacramento. The store features a product line that combines the casual look of a boat shoe with the upscale aesthetic of a man's dress slipper. Each item is handmade by Schwartz in a range of fabrics, including high-quality leather and luxurious Loro Piana cashmere from Italy. The shoes feature leather laces, water-resistant rubber soles and canvas toeboxes for structure and durability. Benjamins Shoes provides the ideal finish to an outfit that needs a precise measure of individuality. Every pair is made in an extremely limited run to ensure the bespoke aura.

**1104 R Street, #130**
benjamins-shoes.com

Inside *R Street*

# LOCALIS

At Localis, chef-owner Christopher Barnum-Dann celebrates Northern California dining in every way: each plate embraces the Sacramento ethos of local sourcing but eschews a rustic presentation in favor of treating every dish like a work of art. Take for example the beet salad: showcasing beets in multiple ways, the dish features ruby red and golden beets, roasted, smoked and pickled, with a light sifting of ingeniously engineered beet "dust." Satisfying homey flavors from roasted octopus, Wagyu beef with mashed potatoes and halibut over coconut curry risotto are a feast for the palate as well as the eye. Pick and choose from the small but well-curated menu or select the five-course chef's tasting menu to sample the best Chef Barnum-Dann and his talented kitchen staff have to offer. If you're lucky enough to snag a seat at the counter, you can even watch the artists at work.

2031 S Street
916.737.7699
localissacramento.com

INSIDE R Street

## HOOK & LADDER MANUFACTURING COMPANY

Hearty appetites and grand ambitions meet and become combustible at Hook & Ladder Manufacturing Company. A former warehouse boasting a proud blue-collar legacy amid corrugated tin and reclaimed wood, Hook & Ladder embraces a lofty vision – it strives to serve as the quintessential Sacramento restaurant and bar. This means an emphasis on locally sourced food and drinks and a menu with inspiration stretching from the Sierra foothills to the Mediterranean. Meals are served all day under the guidance of chef Anthony Scuderi, though dinner offers the widest array. Small plates allow guests to savor crispy pork belly bites or Spanish octopus, plus pizza and entrees that include chicken, pork cassoulet and the celebrated half-pound H&L burger. Chickpea fritters are a lunchtime favorite. The bar excels in creative spirits and can work wonders with rye.

**1630 S Street**
**916. 442.4885**
**hookandladder916.com**

INSIDE R Street

## CAFÉ BERNARDO

Seasonal menus with fresh, locally sourced ingredients and creative bar concepts unique to each Café Bernardo location make these eateries neighborhood favorites from Midtown to the R Street Corridor to Downtown. A cornerstone of Sacramento's legendary Paragary Restaurant Group, Café Bernardo combines an informal, European-style café environment with the quality and attention to detail that have been Randy and Stacy Paragary's standard for decades. Certain favorites endure year round, such as the mushroom, Jarlsberg cheese and parsley salad and Thai noodle salad, which brims with chicken, carrots, cucumbers, scallions and thin noodles in a spicy peanut dressing. Sandwiches are globally inspired and include banh mi, Cubano and mushroom melt. The burgers and pizzettas rate among the best in town. Lines form for weekend breakfast, where fans savor the Bernardo Breakfast Sandwich (two farm eggs, bacon, Romesco, grilled onion and white cheddar with herbed potatoes), amaretto brioche French toast and whole-grain blueberry pancakes.

**1431 R Street**
**916.930.9191**
**paragarys.com**

# MAGPIE CAFÉ

From its first meal in 2009, Magpie Café has defined the term "farm-to-fork." Seasonal menus, locally sourced ingredients and a sustainable environment have been goals consistently met by this ambitious restaurant, which expanded from its R Street home uptown to 16th Street in 2014. Co-owners Ed Roehr and Janel Inouye maintain the original location as a base for their powerhouse catering business (which provided their introduction to the hospitality industry). The new building fits ideally with the Magpie mentality. Called 16 Powerhouse, the space features LEED-certified solar water heating and other green energy features, and Roehr and Inouye link menu items directly to the seasons. Favorites include crispy pork belly, a trio of dragon mushrooms, Pacific Northwest crab and shrimp Louie, a cheese plate sourced from Marin and a Kingbird Farm special for breakfast. Wine, beer and spirits from the Sacramento region and the Bay Area are featured.

**1601 16th Street**
**916.452.7594**
**magpiecafe.com**

# FISH FACE POKE BAR

Hawaiian chefs invented poke as a fresh fish appetizer. Sacramento chef Billy Ngo, whose Kru sushi restaurant took Japanese raw fish delicacies to a new stratosphere, is letting his imagination roam across the deep blue Pacific with Fish Face Poke Bar. Under Ngo's guidance, humble Hawaiian poke breaks free from its appetizer limitations and becomes a complete meal, complex, surprising and satisfying. Every dish of Fish Face Poke is made to order with green and white onions, seaweed, sesame seeds and a choice of proteins—ahi tuna, octopus, shrimp, Ora king salmon, Passmore Ranch sturgeon, scallops, mussels and tofu. The sauces—including sesame soy, spicy kimchi ponzu, wasabi soy, creamy cilantro pesto or yuzu ponzu—make poke unique and imaginative. Fish Face Poke Bar gets the customers into the game by providing ingredients to customize the dish, including cilantro, jalapeño, rice crisps, crunchy garlic, daikon sprouts, macadamia nuts, seasonal fruit, fish roe and seaweed. The bar is stocked with local beers and stellar sake.

**1104 R Street, Suite 100**
**916.706.0605**
**fishfacepokebar.com**

INSIDE R Street

## IRON HORSE TAVERN

One hundred sixty years ago, passenger trains rumbled down R Street from Sacramento to Folsom. Next came freight trains serving endless warehouses. Today, locomotive history merges with industrial cool and the sleek modernity of a revitalized neighborhood at Iron Horse Tavern. This dining destination from the Wong family restaurateurs Mason, Curtis and Alan, Iron Horse features a style that combines industrial and international design. Vintage touches including reclaimed wood and hexagonal tile floors share space. The bar is beautiful, with black anodized steel and a pounded copper top. Blown-glass lighting fixtures, leather banquettes and a model locomotive perched beneath the antique tin ceiling make the atmosphere simultaneously edgy and comfortable. The vibe continues with the gastropub menu overseen by chef Christian Palmos. Iron Horse offers breakfast and brunch, with pancakes, frittatas and eggs, plus salads, sandwiches, pizzas and small plates made with locally sourced produce and a popular macaroni and cheese bar for lunch and dinner. Signature cocktails, beer and wine are available on the patio, which opens to R Street and the city's hippest old and new neighborhood.

1800 15th Street
916.448.4488
ironhorsetavern.net

# SHOKI RAMEN HOUSE

Under the guidance of chef and owner Yasushi Ueyama, ramen becomes a culinary art form that is as much about health and wellbeing as flavor. Following a successful career as a restaurateur and chef in Kobe, Japan, Ueyama and his family arrived in the U.S. in 2001 and opened restaurants in Folsom before founding Shoki Ramen House with co-owner and wife Kathy in Midtown. Ueyama trained at a university as a nutritionist, and wanted to bring the Japanese fine dining style, known as kaiseki, to Sacramento. When kaiseki traditions proved a challenge for local diners, Ueyama shifted to the made-from-scratch, wholesome deliciousness of traditional ramen. Shoki Ramen House broths and dishes include no preservatives or MSG. Ueyama purchases ingredients from local farms and uses cage-free, organic eggs and grass-fed beef in his two famous ramen varieties, Blended (featuring wafu broth, a Japanese traditional soup) and Vegetable, served at a precise temperature to maintain the soup's immense nutrient value.

**1201 R Street**
**2530 21st Street**
**916.454.2411**
**shokiramenhouse.com**

# MEDIUM RARE RECORDS & COLLECTABLES
# KICKSVILLE VINYL & VINTAGE

Travel back to a more innocent—dare we say better?—moment, when entertainment was analog, music was vinyl and long hair was rebellious at MediumRare Records & Collectables. Marty DeAnda (shown standing) created MediumRare in 2010 as diversion from the everyday pressures of his record label, DIG Music. The retail dream transformed into DeAnda's vision of a vinyl record store, combined with a cache of rare memorabilia, on R Street. The shop is a collector's dream, filled with quality vintage vinyl alongside recordings by Sacramento artists and memorabilia from classic rock, soul, jazz and blues acts from the 1950s through the 1980s. The boutique feels like a museum where visitors can take the artifacts home.

Kicksville Vinyl & Vintage is the creation of Tim and Laura Matranga (shown seated). The Vinyl shop features obscure and unusual vinyl records from the 1950's through the 2000's. The Vintage shop a collection of curated items, including unique mid-century, retro and kitsch selections.

**WAL Public Market**
**1104 R Street**
916.442-5344   digmusic.com
916.706.0536   kicksvilleshop.com

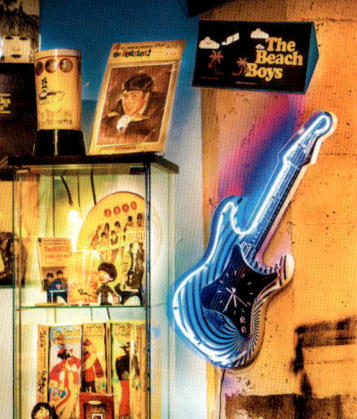

# INSIDE *Midtown*
# INSIDE *Sutter District*

From the Sutter District to Boulevard Park and Poverty Ridge, Midtown not only an offers an intriguing mix of boutiques, bars, galleries and restaurants, but also a collection of smaller neighborhoods.

Historic homes and tree-lined streets invite comfortable strolling and cycling. The mix and density of residential and commercial properties are unique to Sacramento.

The Sutter District is home to many great restaurants and cafes. The area is centered around Sutter's Fort which captures pioneer life at the dawn of the California Gold Rush. John Sutter built the fort as the base of his agricultural empire.

This neighborhood hosts a popular year-round Saturday farmers market creating a vibrant community gathering place. The Second Saturday Art Walk attracts throngs of folks excited by art and creativity.

INSIDE *Sutter District*

# CENTRO COCINA MEXICANA

Regional Mexican cooking inspired by recipes, ingredients and styles rarely found in Sacramento have made Centro Cocina Mexicana a festive Midtown jewel for more than two decades. Paragary Restaurant Group executive chef Kurt Spataro, whose attention to detail and insistence on authenticity have established his legacy as one of Sacramento's most respected chefs, spent months observing kitchens in Mexico's coastal towns and inland cities to prepare the original Centro Cocina Mexicana menu. Repeat journeys have brought new menu items, all faithful to their original geography. Centro's renditions of ceviche de pescado and empanadas, along with tacos, burritos, grilled meats, shrimp and mole, have created a generation of devotees. Centro's colorful atmosphere boasts a constellation of metal star lanterns dangling from the exposed wooden ceiling, decorative crosses and vessels, a vintage motorcycle floating above a window, and touches of pink and blue on the walls. The full-service bar features more than 300 brands of tequila, cold Mexican draft beer and everything in between.

**2730 J Street**
**916.442.2552**
**paragarys.com**

81

INSIDE *Midtown*

## FLEET FEET

Runners across Northern California regard Fleet Feet as a presence far beyond a typical retail sports store. With a deep inventory and personal, expert advice from staffers who share a runner's passion, Fleet Feet is more pro shop than store. Founders Jan and Pat Sweeney say their goal is to "bring our town to its feet," and they mean it. Fleet Feet was founded in Sacramento in 1976 and grew into a nationally franchised operation. Twenty years ago, the Sweeney team bought the original Sacramento store. Time passes and trends change. But the original spirit remains the hallmark of the Fleet Feet shopping experience on J Street. Fleet Feet focuses on shoes and clothing for running and active lifestyles. Completing the Fleet Feet experience is a team of 40 employees, including training divisions that each year help more than 2,500 athletes gain their footing.

**2311 & 2315 J Street**
**916.442.3338**
**fleetfeetsacramento.com**

## PARAGARY'S

A bustling bistro blossomed to life on the edge of Midtown in the summer of 2015, delivered by Sacramento's leading restaurateur in a space he knows intimately well. Randy Paragary, wife Stacy and executive chef Kurt Spataro spent more than a year remodeling the corner of 28th and N streets for the third time since 1975. Four decades ago, the restaurant was a fern bar called Lord Beaverbrook's. A remodel in 1983 brought the namesake Paragary's to 28th Street, which gave way to the current chic new environment of a French-inspired bistro, with intricate black and white encaustic concrete tile floors, simple tables and sleek banquettes that manage to be both quaint and contemporarily cool. The light and airy interiors open to Paragary's renowned patio with waterfalls, 60-year-old olive trees and a fireplace. Spataro brings his precise touch to a menu that delivers California twists on French classics. The croque monsieur sandwich served on toasted brioche with gruyere and Niman Ranch ham is completed by an inspired béchamel sauce. Mary's chicken liver mousse comes with an onion confit and marsala sauce. The wood oven–roasted mussels served with lemon, olive oil, shallots, garlic, herbs and grilled bread are delicious. Their weekend brunch is one of the city's best. Forty years and counting, Paragary's thrives.

**1401 28th Street**
**916.457.5737**
**paragarys.com**

Inside *Midtown*

# SACRAMENTO NATURAL FOODS CO-OP

Every lifestyle—omnivore, vegan, raw, paleo, organic, gluten-free and carnivore—can find sustenance at the Sacramento Natural Foods Co-op. The "Co-op," as fans call the store, was founded as a natural food collective in 1972, a time when organic and natural foods were rare in Sacramento. Today, thousands of members maintain ownership in the co-op, but you don't have to be an owner to enjoy the bountiful selections found along every aisle. The produce department is 100 percent organic. Many items, including honey, olive oil, jams, cheese, wine and beer, are purchased from local producers. Each produce item is marked with the farm name and location where the food was grown. Educational programs encourage the community to cook, eat and live well. There are cooking classes for all ages, wellness workshops led by local health professionals and farm tours. Artisan products are available daily, and the deli has devoted fans lined up at lunchtime. For warehouse shoppers, the co-op carries more than 700 items to purchase in bulk.

2820 R Street
916.455.2667
sac.coop

# SUZIE BURGER

A 1950s burger joint comes alive within a former "Orbit"-style gas station at the corner of 29th and P streets, complete with a pointed roof that looks like it migrated from Mars, circa 1960. Suzie Burger makes the mash-up of eras work like magic in a setting that can never be duplicated, with outstanding, proudly American food to seal the deal. Vintage architecture and clever interior design make Suzie Burger worth the first visit, but return trips will be driven by the namesake burgers, cheesesteaks and other mid-century delights produced by inventive brothers Matt and Fred Haines. Matt is the numbers guy, Fred the chef. The partnership flourishes thanks to high-quality food, starting with 100 percent USDA Choice beef, along with hand-cut fries, the classic Philly cheesesteak, foot-long hot dogs and Suzie's famous Chocolate Brick Sundae. Not exactly what the doctor ordered, but delicious every time.

**2820 P Street**
**916.455.3500**
**suzieburger.com**

# SUN & SOIL JUICE COMPANY

Molly Brown (shown at left) and Tatiana Kaiser opened Sun & Soil in June 2014 with a simple mission: infuse raw, organic nutrition into the community through delicious juice, smoothies and food with produce from local farms. Sun & Soil seeks out the freshest, non-GMO fruits and vegetables to ensure that all drinks are naturally raw, vegan and gluten-free with no processed sugars. Committed to protecting the environment from the inside out, Brown and Kaiser reduce their carbon footprint with a glass bottle exchange program as they move from plastic or Styrofoam options. Sun & Soil specializes in cold-pressed juice, which minimizes heat and the oxidation of nutrients. The process places two tons of pressure onto the pulp to extract the juices. It releases three to five times the amount of micronutrients, enzymes and flavor compared to traditional juicing methods. The cold-press method allows for a shelf life of up to five days, making it easy for customers to enjoy fresh juice as a part of their daily nutrition. Sun & Soil offers an array of flavors and guidance to help reboot digestive systems in most delicious ways. Also featured are organic snacks such as goji bites and house-made granola, served within a quaint, sunshine-yellow storefront.

**1912 P Street**
**916.341.0327**
**sunandsoiljuice.com**

INSIDE *Midtown*

# UNIVERSITY ART

Creativity finds no boundaries at University Art, where plush puppets, notebooks and magnets share shelf space with paintbrushes, pens, charcoal pencils, paper, ink, frames, canvas and paints for every palette. Founded in 1948 by two sisters determined to provide a reasonably priced one-stop shop for artists, sculptors and writers, University Art succeeds far beyond those post-war expectations. Today, University Art honors its founding mission but has expanded to include services as diverse as Sacramento's creative community. The shop offers custom framing and art education materials, along with an array of No. 2 pencils, journals and calendars. Manager David Saalsaa has even turned University Art into a gallery: rotating installations brighten the front window. More than 100 artists have enjoyed showings at University Art, the art store with everything.

**2601 J Street**
**916.443.5721**
**universityart.com**

INSIDE *Midtown*

## THE WATERBOY

Classic European delicacies such as steak tartare, sautéed veal sweetbreads, braised lamb shank and simmering bouillabaisse blend with locally sourced ingredients to make The Waterboy a treasured destination on Sacramento's culinary map. Established in 1996 by homegrown chef and owner Rick Mahan, The Waterboy builds upon the region's farm-to-fork legacy. Mahan gathers the freshest produce, fish and meats to create masterful dishes worthy of a French countryside bistro or a northern Italian ristorante. The chef, whose professional career began at age 16, pairs delicious ingredients and highly polished skills with a diverse wine list and full bar featuring artisanal cocktails and aperitifs. Desserts are made fresh daily. The Waterboy was inspired by a journey Mahan took to France. The chef consistently delivers on his goal to create intriguing European-style fare with California ingredients, no passport needed.

**2000 Capitol Avenue**
**916.498.9891**
**waterboyrestaurant.com**

INSIDE *Sutter District*

## BIBA RISTORANTE ITALIANO

Legendary chef, cookbook author and restaurant owner Biba Caggiano has bustled nonstop between kitchen and dining area, greeting guests and checking pasta dishes at the elegant restaurant for 32 years. Caggiano and husband, Vince, a physician renowned for his work in oncology, have made this special place a component of their home and life. For a generation, Biba has set the standard for professional service—including nightly live piano thanks to musicians Rich O'Day (shown), Claudette Stone and Reggie Graham—the best seasonal ingredients and exquisite preparation and presentation. These days, Vince oversees the wine list while Biba directs the kitchen and front of the house, somehow simultaneously. Born in Bologna, Italy, Biba arrived in Sacramento with her husband in 1969. She entertained friends at home with recipes liberated from her mother's kitchen. She was persuaded to stage informal cooking classes, which expanded to television segments and cookbooks—nine volumes are currently in print. Biba Ristorante and the creative force behind it are both Sacramento treasures.

**2801 Capitol Avenue**
**916.455.2422**
**biba-restaurant.com**

INSIDE *Midtown*

# FEDERALIST PUBLIC HOUSE

Marvin (shown) and Bridgette Maldonado are in pursuit of the perfect pizza. The Florin High School sweethearts and owners of Federalist Public House—the infinitely cool farm-to-fork restaurant in the alley between Capitol Avenue and N Street, 20th and 21st streets—spent a year researching pizza before opening their eatery in December 2014. The couple's three sons served as taste testers. The menu features a variety of signature wood-fired pizzas under the direction of chef Shannon McElroy, plus a rotating selection of local craft beers, wine, nitro coffee and kombucha served at communal tables that run alongside a bocce court. The restaurant and pub are housed in giant steel shipping containers—a design-driven idea from Marvin—in the converted backyard of a Victorian house built in the Federalist style, which inspired the restaurant's name.

**2009 Matsui Alley
916.661.6134
federalistpublichouse.com**

INSIDE *Midtown*

## BLOCK BUTCHER BAR

Snug, friendly and warm, Block Butcher Bar is the meat, whiskey and wine hideaway established by entrepreneur Michael Hargis next to his LowBrau beer emporium. The two locations could not be more different in appearance, ambition and style, but they operate in complete harmony and thrive within their contrasting environments. Block Butcher Bar is a hearty boutique that celebrates the butcher's art while paying homage to the distiller—the selection of brown spirits is astonishing. More than 160 single-malt and blended Scotch, Irish and American rye and whiskey options stand ready for enjoyment. The menu includes house-cured charcuterie, artisanal cheeses, signature sandwiches and seasonal bites. The sausage is made fresh daily and spiced to European perfection.

**1050 20th Street**
**916.476.6306**
**blockbutcherbar.com**

INSIDE *Midtown*

# LUMENS LIGHT & LIVING

A dazzling collection of ceiling lights, indoor and outdoor wall sconces, table lamps, floor lamps, architectural lighting and all objects illuminative captivate and inspire across a 4,000-square-foot showroom at Lumens Light & Living. Styles are as varied as the hardware, with Arts & Crafts, contemporary, mid-century modern and modern represented among the thousands of lighting options. In a commitment to support independent and emerging artists, founders Ken Plumlee (shown at left) and Peter Weight created space within the showroom for artisan lighting alongside designs from brands such as Alessi, Kartell and Philippe Starck. The Lumens team of lighting experts can help with technical specifications and design plans to bring a homeowner's ideas to completion. And the best designs in modern home and personal accessory products are featured in their Design Shop within the store. Also worthy of a visit is Lumens Annex at 712 R Street, where clearance and open-box items are offered.

**2028 K Street**
**916.444.5585**
**lumens.com**

INSIDE *Sutter District*

# THE RED RABBIT KITCHEN & BAR

Owners Matt Nurge and John Bays—who serve as barman and chef, respectively—focus on all things local at The Red Rabbit. They present food served with boundless sophistication and local ingredients and run an endlessly bespoke operation, making as much as possible by hand. Appropriately, even the syrups for The Red Rabbit's creative cocktails are created in-house. The juices are fresh-squeezed and the herbs are hand-muddled. Even the wines are a celebration of California's hands-on viticulture. With a space that manages to be cool, industrial, warm and welcoming at once, The Red Rabbit provides comfort from the moment a customer arrives. The lighting is low, the wood mellow and dark, and the brick walls are well aged. The menu is an eclectic mix of classics with a twist—pork belly kimchi tacos, fried Brussels sprouts and bacon, beet carpaccio, rabbit Bolognese, vegan mushroom potato curry. Brunch and happy hour presentations are exceedingly popular.

2718 J Street
916.706.2275
theredrabbit.net

# PUBLIC ART

Framed by two rivers with the Sierra Nevada and Coast Ranges rising on its horizons, Sacramento is blessed with natural beauty. Today, the creative arts are supplementing the community's natural treasures, and Sacramento is increasingly recognized for public artworks that surprise, inspire and delight. Dozens of public art installations can be found while strolling in neighborhoods across the city's grid. Monumental and intimate works can be discovered along streets, in buildings and parks throughout the community. These artworks celebrate the culture of the city and contribute to Sacramento's uniqueness. The works are possible because Sacramento is home to a "percent for art" program that reserves a portion of construction dollars from civic development projects for public art. The result is the "Art in Public Places" program, administered by the Sacramento Metropolitan Arts Commission. The program is committed to expanding the public's knowledge and experience of the visual arts. Maps are available with directions to most of the major permanent artworks on display downtown. Multiple blocks are described, but tours can be broken into easily manageable mini-treks of artistic discovery.

916.808.3992
sacmetroarts.org

# MIDTOWN FARMERS MARKET

Each Saturday morning from 8 A.M. to 1 P.M., the Midtown Farmers Market transforms the outdoor community center of the historic and eclectic Midtown neighborhood. Dozens of vendors with fresh, locally grown and frequently organic produce and flowers blend with numerous artisanal food sellers. Shoppers wander and sample regionally produced honey, fresh almond milk, zesty beef jerky and hand-rolled pastas. A mini food truck prepares Belgian waffles. Barbequed meats are grilled and smoked to fall off the bone as local residents and visitors enjoy their meals at nearby picnic tables. Kombucha and juices made fresh in the neighborhood are available as finishing touches. Children play in a dedicated area called the Budding Foodies zone. Musical artists perform while crowds gather, make purchases and linger in the relaxed, informal fellowship the Midtown Farmers Market brings to the neighborhood.

**20th and J Streets**
exploremidtown.org

Inside *Midtown*

## TAPA THE WORLD

Traditional Spanish and Basque tapas, live music and inspired cocktails are a tradition at Tapa the World, founded in 1994 by siblings Conni Levis and Paul Ringstrom. Conni Levis is shown here with executive chef Marcos Murillo (center) and bar manager Chris Callaway (right). This lively restaurant offers a sophisticated assortment of small-plate dishes to be shared and savored. Tapa the World is popular for *la comida* (lunch) and *la cena* (dinner)

and all the *bebidas* (drinks) and *postres* (desserts) in between. A typical Tapa the World adventure begins with tortilla Española (the "Spanish poor man's" potato cake cooked in olive oil with onion and egg), followed by jamon Serrano (dry cured and aged Spanish ham) and champiñones al ajillo (mushrooms sautéed in olive oil, garlic, parsley and white wine). From there, aceitunas (a selection of olives from Spain and around the world) serves as an interlude, with patatas bravas (fried potato cubes with spicy tomato sauce), calamares fritos (calamari dusted with Spanish pimentón and lightly fried with Romesco sauce), and berenjenas (eggplant, breaded and fried, topped with a cool tomato, garlic and herb compote and shredded Parmesan) to follow, all at a relaxing pace. The house-made sangria is direct from Iberia.

2115 J Street
916.442.4353
tapatheworld.com

# Inside Midtown

## HABERDASHERIE

Combine a love of shopping with a dream to operate a retail store. The result is Ruthie McRonald and Haberdasherie at 23rd and J streets. McRonald transitioned from a married, stay-at-home mom to a wine industry expert to a gift shop owner when she christened Haberdasherie in April 2017. McRonald spends hours each day searching for interesting items to bring to her shelves, often with the help of a friend. The women peruse markets from Los Angeles to Paris while curating the store's eclectic mix of gifts and sensibilities. Treasures include candles, hostess items, napkins, pillows, tea towels, throws, vases, tea sets, beach bags and original art. The inventory is always changing, which fits the whimsical name Haberdasherie, a word used in Europe for sewing notions and clothing. A dictionary would insist on spelling the shop's name "haberdashery," but McRonald changed it "because I like it that way."

**2318 J Street**
**916.215.7444**
**haberdasherie.net**

INSIDE *Midtown*

## LOWBRAU

Beer – gallons of it – serves as the foundation at 1050 20th Street, but there's much more to LowBrau than cold German pilsner or lager. The creativity of Midtown restaurateur Michael Hargis stretches from Sacramento to Munich at this modern version of the classic German bierhalle. The feast begins with Bavarian pretzels and moves swiftly to savory meats, including pork, chicken or lamb sausages. There are sandwiches highlighted by pastrami, turkey and schnitzel, and meat and cheese boards, which combine favorites from France, Spain and Germany. The specialty meats are prepared next door at Block Butcher Bar. LowBrau is an experience that summarizes Midtown Sacramento: quirky and seriously delicious.

1050 20th Street
916.706.2636
lowbrausacramento.com

INSIDE *Midtown*

## SKOOL JAPANESE GASTROPUB

Catching the wave of izakaya-style Japanese restaurants launched Skool successfully to the forefront of unique Sacramento dining experiences. At first look, there's nothing overly exotic about izakaya – it refers to convivial, informal dining and drinking and small dishes, not unlike tapas or an Irish pub. But Skool is nothing like your neighborhood sushi bar. Since its opening at 23rd and K streets, Skool Japanese Gastropub has streamlined its delectable menu in a space that features fun, kitschy colors. Meals range from oysters, sardines and sashimi to chicken and beef. The experience should be savored without hurry. The sake selection is impressive with at least 10 drink options, and the bar specializes in Japanese Chu-Hi cocktails – fresh, seasonal fruit drinks made with shochu, a spirit similar to vodka. Don't overlook the weekend brunch, which features an Osaka-style take on chicken and waffles.

2319 K Street
916.737.5767
skoolonkstreet.com

# REVOLUTION WINES

As the city's only fully operational urban winery, Revolution Wines is devoted to the idea that locally produced wine and food is the best expression of the Sacramento landscape, or terroir. Revolution is owned by Gina Genshlea (shown) and her husband, Joe. From its headquarters on S Street, Revolution excels as a full-service operation, combining the winery, tasting room and eatery in one location. Using fruit from Yolo Vineyards, Aparicio Vineyards, Gandyhill Vineyards and Sutter Ranch Vineyards, Revolution's family-owned and -operated facility crushes, ferments and bottles in the city's midst. The sophisticated kitchen offers Italian classics such as fritto misto, an antipasto plate and a steak panzanella salad. Heartier fare is also available, such as steak frites and Prince Edward Island mussels, to complement exclusive wine pairings for oenophiles and foodies alike.

2831 S Street
916.444.7711
rev.wine

# TRUE

"Fashion for Good" is the motive and motto behind TRUE boutique in Midtown. TRUE stands for Totally Recycled Urban Exchange. The concept for the 2,350-square-foot retail clothing boutique was established in 2015 by WEAVE, Women Escaping a Violent Environment, the nonprofit organization that serves as the primary provider of crisis intervention services for survivors of domestic violence and sexual assault in Sacramento County. One hundred percent of proceeds earned through the buying, selling and trading of fashion items at TRUE fund programs and services to empower survivors of domestic violence and sexual assault. The goal is for WEAVE clients to regain independence and live their lives free of violence. The shop features clothing, shoes and accessories. TRUE customers contribute to making the community a better and safer place for hundreds of local women, men and children.

1900 K Street
916.643.4606
trueclothing.org

INSIDE *Midtown*

# TEMPLE COFFEE ROASTERS

After returning home from a lengthy stay in Indonesia, Temple founder and barista Sean Kohmescher opened the first Temple Coffee house on S Street in 2005. His dream was to create a gathering place, much like the temples he visited in his travels. His vision was simple. Good vibe, great service and exceptionally well-prepared coffee. Over the past 12 years, the vision has grown to include five coffee houses and a roastery that prepares the delectable bean juice used at each Temple location and sold to restaurants around the region. The roastery holds monthly coffee education courses on home brewing, tasting and espresso preparation, and free weekly tastings. In keeping with its "farm to cup" sustainable coffee sourcing philosophy, Temple's director of coffee, Eton Tsuno, travels six to eight months a year to meet coffee producers and build sustainable, direct relationships with farms. Temple was named a top coffee roaster in the U.S. by CNN and *Fortune* magazine.

**2200 K Street**
**916.662.7625**

**2829 S Street**
**916.454.1272**

**1010 9th Street**
**916.443.4960**
**templecoffee.com**

# INSIDE *the Handle*

The Handle District, tucked between downtown and Midtown, is the city's smallest neighborhood.

Yet it includes an exciting group of restaurants, bars, nightclubs and retail businesses in the area bounded by 18th and 19th streets, L Street and Capitol Avenue. It is also home to one of the city's most activated alleys.

Interesting historic commercial buildings, restored Victorians and newly designed apartment homes sit comfortably side by side and give the neighborhood an eclectic feel on easily walkable city streets.

The Handle is also home to Sacramento's Walk of Stars, and host to numerous events including Second Saturdays, fashion shows, farm-to-fork festivals and a celebration on Bastille Day.

INSIDE *the Handle*

## GINGER ELIZABETH CHOCOLATES

Pure bittersweet chocolate ganache. Liquid caramel punctuated by fleur de sel. Almond praline with crunchy croquant. The display cases at Ginger Elizabeth Chocolates reveal a world of sweet sophistication unmatched in Sacramento. Formally trained chocolatier and pastry chef Ginger Elizabeth Hahn and her husband, Tom (who manages the business), have created a decadent hot spot, selling delicious items made from the finest ingredients. Specializing in bonbons, pralines, caramels, dessert bars and macarons, Ginger Elizabeth celebrates the venerable craft of chocolate guided by principles of freshness. Those principles are apparent in every bite. All products at Ginger Elizabeth are natural and contain no preservatives. The subtle sheen of the tempered chocolate is never dyed or artificially colored. The couverture chocolate is carefully culled from top-notch cacao sources. All dairy products are certified humane. And Ginger Elizabeth favors recyclable or compostable packaging made domestically. Ginger Elizabeth is chocolate at its finest.

1801 L Street
916.706.1738
gingerelizabeth.com

INSIDE *the Handle*

## SCOUT LIVING

Sacramento boasts a significant collection of mid-century modern architecture. Thanks to Scout Living, residents can find the furniture and accessories to match. Scout Living is an antique and design collective that celebrates more than 20 of the finest dealers in Northern California. They specialize in rare and vintage treasures from across the decades, but the emphasis is on mid-century modern, Danish modern and vintage furniture. Owners Erin Boyle and Stefan Betz Bloom brought their curated vision from their store in San Francisco, and today the local collective is unmatched for sophisticated style. The large brick building brims not only with furniture, but offers vintage clothing, accessories and locally produced craft pieces. The inventory changes daily.

1215 18th Street
916.594.7971
scoutliving.com

# ART OF TOYS

Terri Rehg began collecting toys when she was five years old. Yet the name of her shop only hints at the depth and diversity of her remarkable talent for gathering fun and artistic treasures. Art of Toys presents a precisely edited collection of vintage toys and playthings for kids, especially around the holidays. But Rehg's real claim to fame is the stunning local and international art that fills her 425-square-foot specialty shop. Visual and tactile gifts on display at Art of Toys include remarkable paintings and art works, unusual jewelry and unique sculptures. The inventory reflects Rehg's career, which ranged from serving as a sales manager for a line of New Zealand sheepskin toys, to 14 years in the wholesale toy trade and working in sales for Disney collectibles. When Rehg served as guest curator for an art show at the California History Museum, her dream of opening a store to combine all of her interests took flight. Her extensive website and cozy shop hold endless wonders, from artwork that rotates on a regular basis to gifts and desk decorations. Rehg has a simple definition for the Art of Toys. She describes the shop's merchandise as "tchotchkes of all kinds."

1126 18th Street
916.446.0673
artoftoys.com

# THE RIND

Three simple words encompass the philosophy of The Rind: "Cheese. Wine. Beer." The cheese-centric bar in the Handle District offers artisanal cheeses paired with wines and beers selected by the two certified sommeliers and one certified cicerone—beer taster—on staff. Cheese enthusiasts explore all variety of exotic cheese products, from buttery and blue to nutty and stinky—created from local dairy sources. After sampling an array of slices, customers indulge their imaginations with "grown up" versions of grilled cheese sandwiches and mac and cheese. There are special discounts for "Legen-Dairy Hour," The Rind's version of happy hour. Sara Arbabian, who co-owns the shop with her husband, beer enthusiast Steve Tatterson, has made it her mission to offer locals the experience of a farm-to-fork wine bar without all the fuss and with a focus on fresh ingredients. The result is a tribute to what it means to live and eat well in Sacramento. The Rind features homemade morabas, or preserves, in flavors such as kumquat, pear and cardamom and quince. Each jar is handmade by Sherean Arbabian, The Rind's official "Resident Chef Mother."

**1801 L Street**
**916.441.7463**
**therindsacramento.com**

INSIDE *the Handle*

# MULVANEY'S BUILDING & LOAN

Patrick Mulvaney is serious when he says, "Whatever comes in the front door goes on your plate." A leader of the local farm-to-fork revolution, Mulvaney and his wife, Bobbin, built their reputations around the farm-fresh ingredients and local produce that comprise his masterful Chef's Menus. The offerings at Mulvaney's Building & Loan change daily to accommodate the harvests and the seasons. The chef's New American cuisine features complex and delectable dishes like charcuterie, veal sweetbread bruschetta and brace of stuffed quail. Lunch favorites include the open-faced pork scaloppini sandwich with mustard aioli and pickled vegetables. The gastronomic magic comes together in a converted 1893 firehouse. Brick walls, exposed ductwork and repurposed firehouse doors-as-windows give the restaurant a celebratory vibe that blends into a garden patio. Through the leafy adjacent courtyard stands Next Door, Mulvaney's banquet hall. Next Door features two rooms with bow truss redwood ceilings. The rooms seat 30 or 100 guests, with fine dining assured.

1215 19th Street
916.441.6022
mulvaneysbl.com

INSIDE *the Handle*

# ZOCALO

Towering ceilings and expansive windows beckon natural light and make the inside and outside worlds blend seamlessly at Zocalo. Next comes the décor: mammoth urns, intricate iron works, slab tables and stunning tableware create a culturally stimulating atmosphere for the food and drinks that follow. Housed in the handsomely renovated Arnold Brothers building, which served as a Hudson car dealership in the 1920s, Zocalo's eccentric interior is inspired by the majestic town square of Mexico City, a gathering spot for centuries that embraces its past while embarking toward the future. The food is fresh and colorful, with delightful twists on Mexican menu staples such as queso fundido, empanadas, quesadillas, ceviche, enchiladas and exceptional guacamole. The Cadillac margarita is popular with the bar crowd. Zocalo's massive bar features TV monitors and romantic booths. An expansive patio completes the indoor-outdoor experiences and overlooks Capitol Avenue.

1801 Capitol Avenue
916.441.0303
zocalosacramento.com

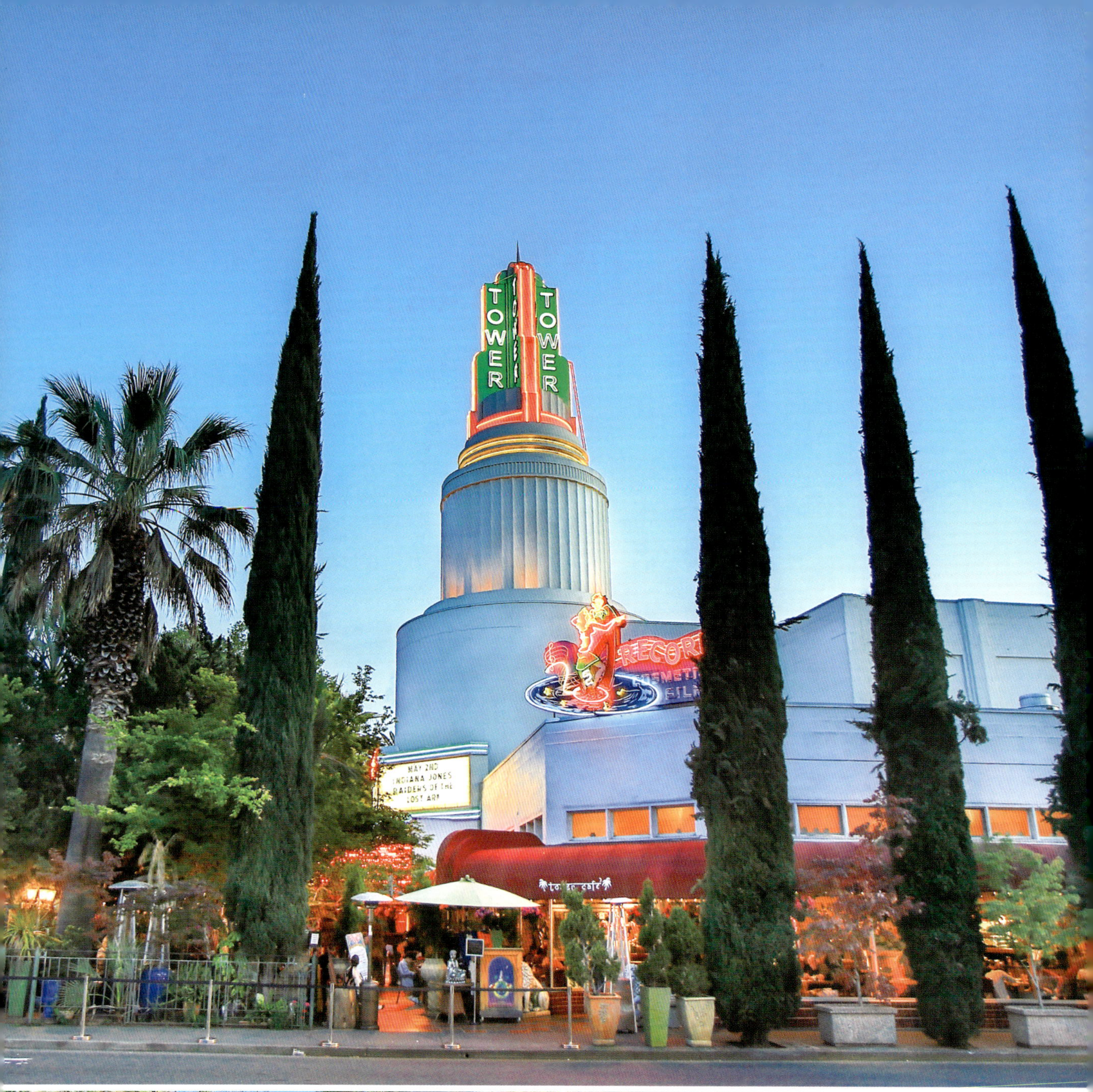
TOWER
TOWER
MAY 2ND
INDIANA JONES
RAIDERS OF THE

WPA
ROCK GARDEN
EST 1940

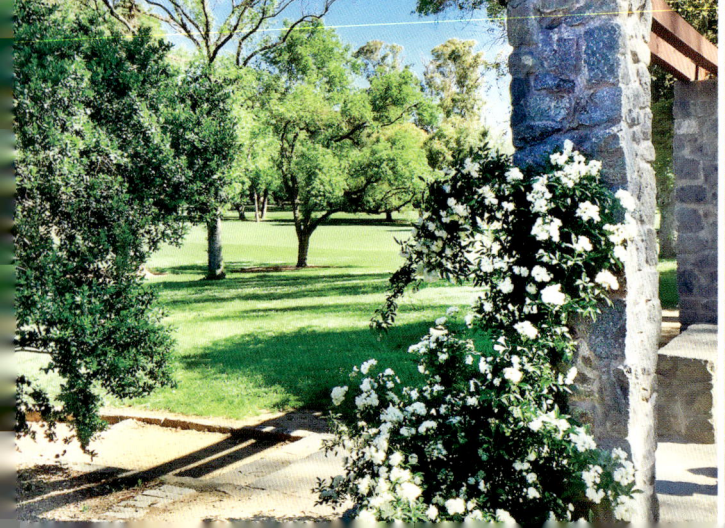

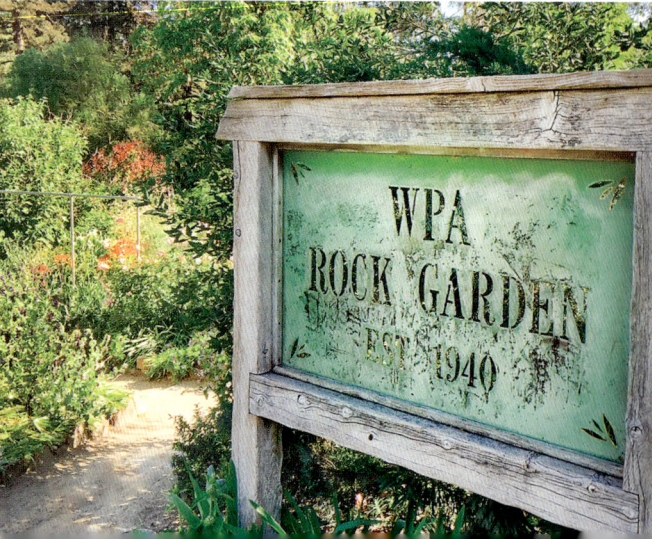

# INSIDE Land & Curtis Parks

Here you find historic homes, tree-lined streets and vibrant City College campus life, along with William Land Park, the city's largest urban park which is home to a golf course, WPA Rock Garden, Fairytale Town and a boutique zoo. Summertime brings the Sacramento Shakespeare Festival to the park's amphitheatre.

Shops and eateries are located in the vibrant Broadway District, home to the historic Tower Theater, the Old City Cemetery, Sacramento Historic Rose Garden and the original Tower Records location (now a bookstore.)

Curtis Park is located east of the City College and has an eclectic collection of historic home styles and a lively park scene. South Land Park is known for its rolling hills and midcentury vibe. Hollywood Park features affordable homes for family-oriented living.

INSIDE *Land Park*

# FAIRYTALE TOWN

Humpty Dumpty's pint-sized gates welcome more than 230,000 guests each year at Fairytale Town, placing the iconic park among the region's top destinations for younger audiences. Since 1959, the Land Park play zone has stood proud and unique with its timeless blend of imaginative architecture and hands-on activities. Supported primarily by public donations and attendance, Fairytale Town builds upon its half-century of success with educational programs and literary connections to inspire new generations. Today, Fairytale Town alumni treat their grandchildren to tours of the Yellow Brick Road and the Crooked Mile. They hitch rides on Cinderella's Coach and hold court in King Arthur's Castle. The park annually welcomes guests from more than 30 California counties and provides inclusive fun for kids from every socioeconomic background and neighborhood. Free admission is provided to low-income children and disabled youngsters, ensuring a positive, enriching experience for everyone.

**3901 Land Park Drive**
**916.808.7462**
**fairytaletown.org**

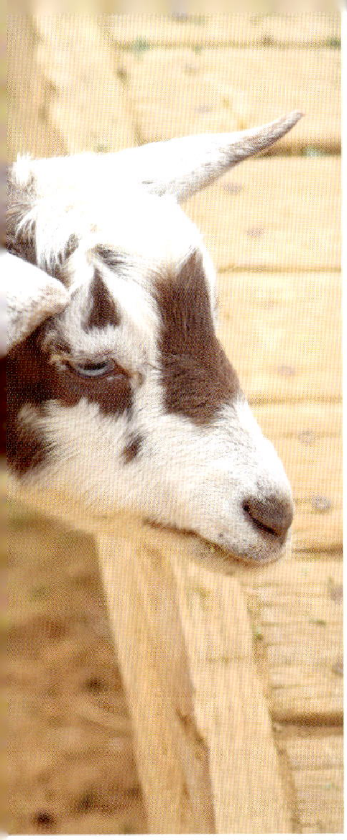

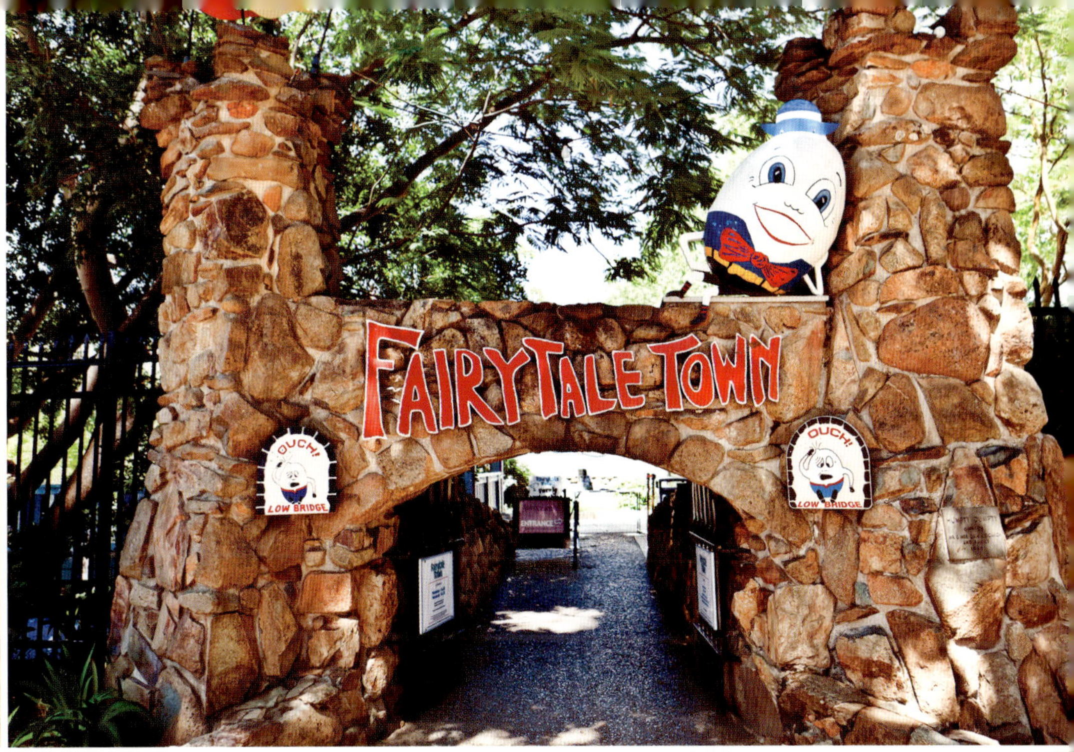

INSIDE *Land Park*

# SACRAMENTO ZOO

Nature comes alive at the Sacramento Zoo. Like its residents and guests, the zoo has evolved in purpose and stature over a history that spans 89 years. When the facility opened in 1927, its name was William Land Park Zoo. There were 40 animals, including monkeys, raccoons, birds, deer and other small animals. Today, the zoo features a menagerie of more than 500 birds, mammals and reptiles living on 14.2 acres. Emphasis is on conservation, education, appreciation and respect for these unique creatures who share our community. Among the exotics are the reticulated giraffe, Grevy's zebra, ring-tailed lemur, African lion, giant anteater and many more. The Sacramento Zoo is an oasis where guests wander shaded pathways and view nature from a perspective designed along organic, interactive lines. The zoo is the perfect location for personal meditation and youthful inspiration in the heart of the city.

**3930 W. Land Park Drive**
**916.808.5888**
**saczoo.org**

INSIDE *Land Park*

# FREEPORT BAKERY

A passion for baking brought a sweet life to Marlene and Walter Goetzeler. As co-owners of Freeport Bakery for the past 28 years, the Goetzelers share a love of baking forged the first day they met. The story might have been written for Hollywood. Walter, raised by a prominent baking family in Bavaria, wandered into a San Diego bookshop run by Marlene. He was looking for a map. She wanted a German tutor. The fit was perfect. Love blossomed. Decades later, the duo dishes up incredible specialty cakes and delicious desserts—including Danish pastries, muffins, pies, cookies and savory items—from scratch at their full-line bakery with the help of 50 staff members. Freeport Bakery is an iconic Land Park location with a vintage-inspired interior detailed with as much care as the baked goods they create. Customers drive miles to retrieve custom orders. On top of all that, Marlene serves as president of the Retail Bakers of America, which offers hands-on workshops, bakery tours, educational classes, local vendor displays and annual road shows to connect baking aficionados across the country.

**2966 Freeport Boulevard**
**916.442.4256**
**freeportbakery.com**

INSIDE *Land Park*

# RIVERSIDE CLUBHOUSE

There were no shortcuts to success in repurposing the old dive bar Hereford House on Riverside Boulevard in Land Park. The dump hadn't been updated in decades. The neglect required a massive overhaul to produce a beautiful new culinary destination. Today, the Riverside Clubhouse is the pride of Land Park, another victory for owners Matt and Fred Haines. With a menu built upon traditional American classics and a setting unrivaled, Riverside Clubhouse features a 30-foot wall of water and a three-tiered fireplace on the lovely, secluded patio. There are three 50-inch plasma TV monitors and a spectacular "burning crystal" fireplace in the lounge, which is among the most popular in town. Short ribs, cheesy grits, fish tacos and a killer Cubano sandwich provide alternatives to a classic assortment of burgers. The old Hereford cow from generations forgotten watches over the front door.

**2633 Riverside Boulevard**
**916.448.9988**
**riversideclubhouse.com**

INSIDE *Land Park*

## TAYLOR'S MARKET & KITCHEN

Opened in 1962 by Roy Taylor and Ed Schell, Taylor's Market is a gem in the residential neighborhood where Land Park and Curtis Park meet. The subsequent generation of owners, Ed's son Kevin and friend Danny Johnson (hired as a butcher at age 19 in 1983) dedicated themselves to Taylor's reputation for service and quality. A remodel in 1988 brought new displays for local produce, fine wines and the best meats and seafood in town, plus partnership with local produce purveyor Aki Kushida and son Bruce, who still manages the fresh produce department. Roots run deep among the staff. Store manager Dave Hunter was 17 when he went to work at Taylor's. Meat department manager Paul Carras grew up in the neighborhood and started his career at age 15. Felicia Johnson, daughter of owners Danny and Kathy Johnson, is Taylor's cheese monger. Next door, Taylor's Kitchen features a seasonal menu created by chef Justin Lower with a focus on fresh local foods. Desserts are created in-house. The wine list is selected by master sommelier candidate Keith Fergel. Part market, part fine dining, Taylor's is a Sacramento icon.

**2900 & 2924 Freeport Boulevard**
**916.443.5154**
**taylorskitchen.com**
**916.443.6881**
**taylorsmarket.com**

# HISTORIC ROSE GARDEN

History and horticulture come to life in Sacramento's Old City Cemetery. The Historic Rose Garden was founded in 1992 as a place where roses from historic locations throughout the Mother Lode and beyond could be preserved, studied and enjoyed. The garden, which reaches peak bloom in early spring, has grown to 500 old roses of various types, including plants that no longer exist elsewhere. Planted and maintained by volunteers whose efforts are led by curator Anita Clevenger, the Historic Rose Garden and adjacent cemetery gardens demonstrate how a group of concerned citizens can transform an overrun, neglected city cemetery back into a showplace reminiscent of Victorian times. The Old City Cemetery includes perennial and native plant gardens maintained by volunteers. The Historic Rose Garden has received international honors, including the World Federation of Rose Societies' prestigious "Garden of Excellence" award. People visit from around the world to see the gardens, as well as the monuments of Sacramento pioneers at the Old City Cemetery.

**1000 Broadway**
**916.448.0811**
**historicoldcitycemetery.com**

# CASA GARDEN RESTAURANT

Very rarely can guests enjoy outstanding food in a gorgeous garden setting while contributing to a local charity. Casa Garden Restaurant provides the setting and the opportunity. Since 1973, Casa Garden and its event space, brightened by garden views from every window, have featured a rotating weekly menu created by master chefs. Specials have included sausage and ratatouille over linguine, salsa verde pork enchiladas and grilled romaine with shrimp, followed by decadent desserts like raspberry pie, caramel pecan cheesecake and strawberry margarita torte. This remarkable restaurant is run entirely by volunteers from the Los Niños Service League to raise funds for the Sacramento Children's Home, a nonprofit organization that provides life-changing programs and counseling services for children and families in need. Thanks to the amazing menus designed by the Casa Garden chefs and the tireless work of hundreds of volunteers, nearly $2.9 million has benefited the Sacramento Children's Home over the past four decades.

**2760 Sutterville Road**
**916.452.2809**
**casagarden.org**

INSIDE *Land Park*

## VIC'S ICE CREAM & CAFE

Family owned since 1947, this Land Park heritage spot has been the site of postgame celebrations, report card rewards and summertime gab sessions for more than 70 years. Along with the traditional ice cream parlor favorites such as sundaes, shakes, cups and cones in 29 familiar flavors, Vic's offers an array of American diner classics, including corned beef, tuna and egg salad sandwiches, the Krautdog and Cheezedog, and daily soup specials. The menu shifts with the seasons, but the popular dogs are always available. The Vic's experience expanded three years ago with Vic's Café, located next door to the original ice cream shop. The café features an expanded menu with burritos, entrée salads, pulled pork sliders and baked goods, plus beer and coffee beverages, including a classic espresso. The original Vic's hasn't changed much since its grand opening in 1947 when current owner Craig Rutledge's father, Ash, and buddy Vic Zito—for whom the diner is named—banded together to open the ice cream business of their dreams. The counter stools, black-and-white checkered linoleum floor and blue jean uniforms all speak to Vic's rich history and Land Park legacy. The shop makes its specialty treats available for takeaway to parties and celebrations.

**3199 Riverside Boulevard**
**916.448.0892**
**vicsicecream.com**

**3193 Riverside Boulevard**
**916.475.1223**
**cafevics.com**

## SELLAND'S MARKET-CAFE ON BROADWAY

Nearly two decades after Randall Selland and Nancy Zimmer opened their first Selland's Market-Café in East Sacramento, the new Broadway location brings the chefs' renowned fast-casual sophistication and endlessly creative menu to the city's global food boulevard. The Broadway location was inspired by a modern farmhouse style with high ceilings, floor-to-ceiling windows and a bustling display kitchen. The menu includes American classic dishes from their family recipes featuring homemade meatloaf, chicken breasts smothered in mushroom gravy, cottage pie and barbecued brisket. You can also enjoy a goat cheese and apple salad, wood-fired sausage and mushroom pizza, roast beef sandwich or the signature beef and bean chili. On Sundays, an additional brunch menu includes favorites such as smoked salmon Benedict, eggs Florentine pizza, brioche breakfast sandwiches, avocado tartine, French toast casserole, biscuits and gravy, as well as mimosas, bellinis and champagne bottle service. A must try is the weekly and rotating $25 Dinner for Two special that includes two entrees and a bottle of wine.

915 Broadway
916.732.3390
sellands.com

# WILLIE'S BURGERS

Willie's is a quirky burger joint specializing in timeless classics that made drive-ins and diners famous. The menu is full of traditional favorites such as onion rings, chili cheese fries, milkshakes and big, juicy hamburgers. Owner Bill Taylor, a Land Park native and the "Willie" for whom the restaurant is named, made it his mission to offer locals a serious burger joint. The community responded by making Willie's one of the most successful burger operations in town. Taylor perfected his skills while spending time at the legendary Tommy's in Los Angeles. He took his hibachi with him wherever he went after learning to cook in the National Guard. With three locations—the original right off Broadway, a second in Arden-Arcade and a new third space in Old Sacramento headed by Taylor's son Greg and Greg's wife, Rachel Glabe Taylor—Willie's ensures there's always a burger within reach.

2415 16th Street
110 K Street
916.573.3897
williesburgers.com

# IRON GRILL

Broadway and 13th Street is an unpretentious corner of the city where a simple sign beckons diners to a steakhouse mecca. The sign says "Iron." Behind the doors is a restaurant devoted to hearty eating, with emphasis on red meat traditions such as a 16-ounce New York steak or eight-ounce filet mignon. The mastermind behind Iron Grill is Bill Taylor, the founder of Willie's Burgers. Iron was originally conceived as a casual, neighborhood steakhouse but has evolved into an exceptional foodie attraction with abundant menu choices created by chef Keith Swiryn. Bottomless mimosas and spicy Bloody Mary wake-ups enhance the breakfast experience, along with buttermilk pancakes and omelets. Iron has a full bar, which is sleek and popular with locals from nearby Land Park.

**2422 13th Street**
**916.737.5115**
**irongrillsacramento.com**

# INSIDE Oak Park

The city's first suburb is a history-rich and diverse community on the rebound. Many of Oak Park's historic residences were built before World War II.

The Broadway Triangle is home to more than 60 new urban-style homes and apartments, restaurants and locally owned shops. The monthly Gather event attracts folks from all over to enjoy the neighborhood ambiance.

From the beautifully renovated McClatchy Park and Guild Theater in the 40 Acres complex to the historic properties and bike-friendly streets, this is likely the most interesting place to live, work and play in the city.

INSIDE *Oak Park*

# DISPLAY: CALIFORNIA

Roshaun Davis and his wife Maritza founded the events marketing agency Unseen Heroes to help neighborhood businesses promote events and inventories. That was 2008. Today, the mission has expanded into a creative Oak Park gathering place where local residents shop and connect with their community. Under the name DISPLAY: California, the 850-square-foot retail space provides room for revolving pop-up shops every four to eight weeks, bringing renewed energy to the emerging Triangle District. Inspired by pop-up shops in New York, Los Angeles and San Francisco, DISPLAY has one essential difference. Instead of setting up shop in a temporary space that disappears along with the inventory when the pop-up closes, the Davis family created a permanent space to house a constantly evolving concept. The shop features seasonal themes. "Holladay" was precisely that—unique holiday options from top California designers with apparel, toys, jewelry, beauty and body care products, home accessories and décor. The springtime store, "Bodega," featured artisanal food, kitchen goods and household items in a quaint general store atmosphere. Nothing is ever the same at DISPLAY: California.

**3433 Broadway**
**916.822.4925**
displaycalifornia.com

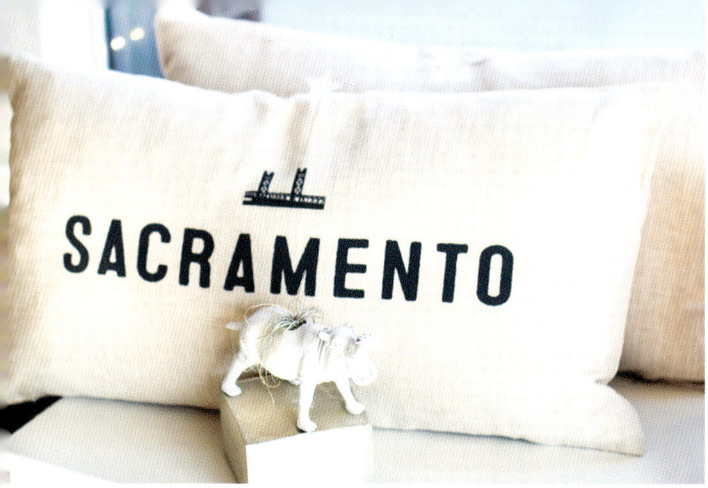
SACRAMENTO

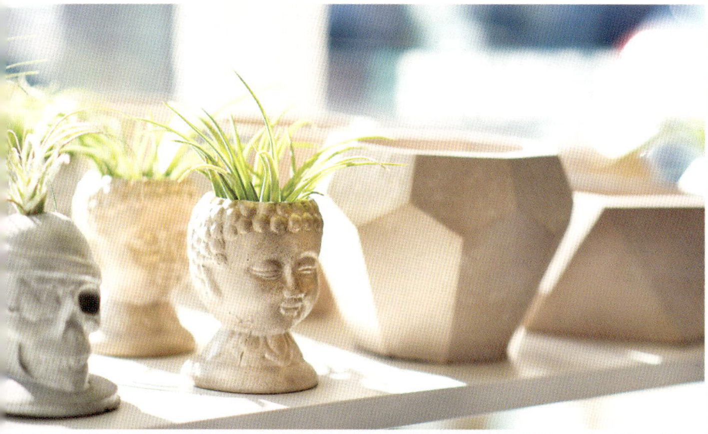

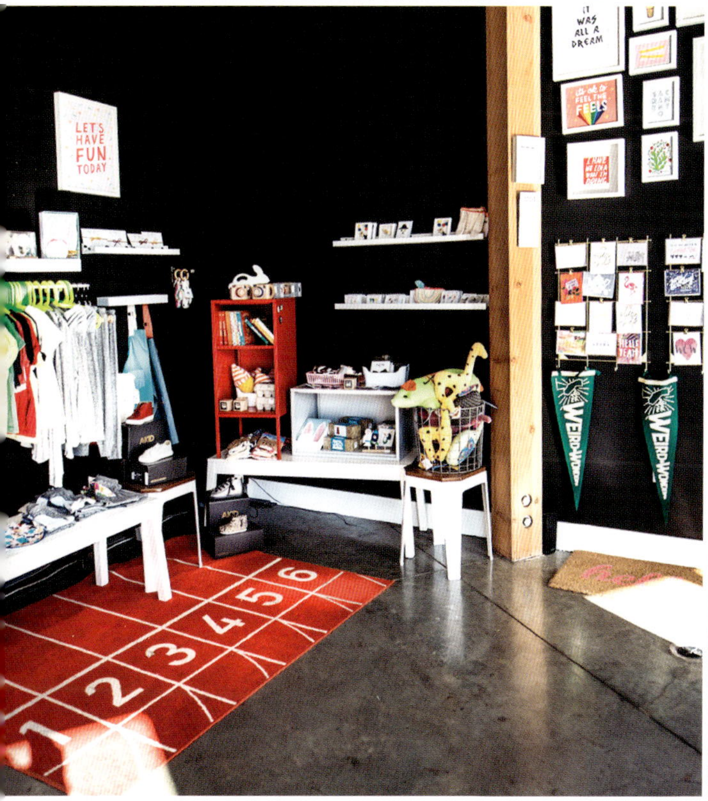
LET'S HAVE FUN TODAY
IT WAS ALL A DREAM

California
SACRAMENTO CALIFORNIA USA

LET'S ADVENTURE

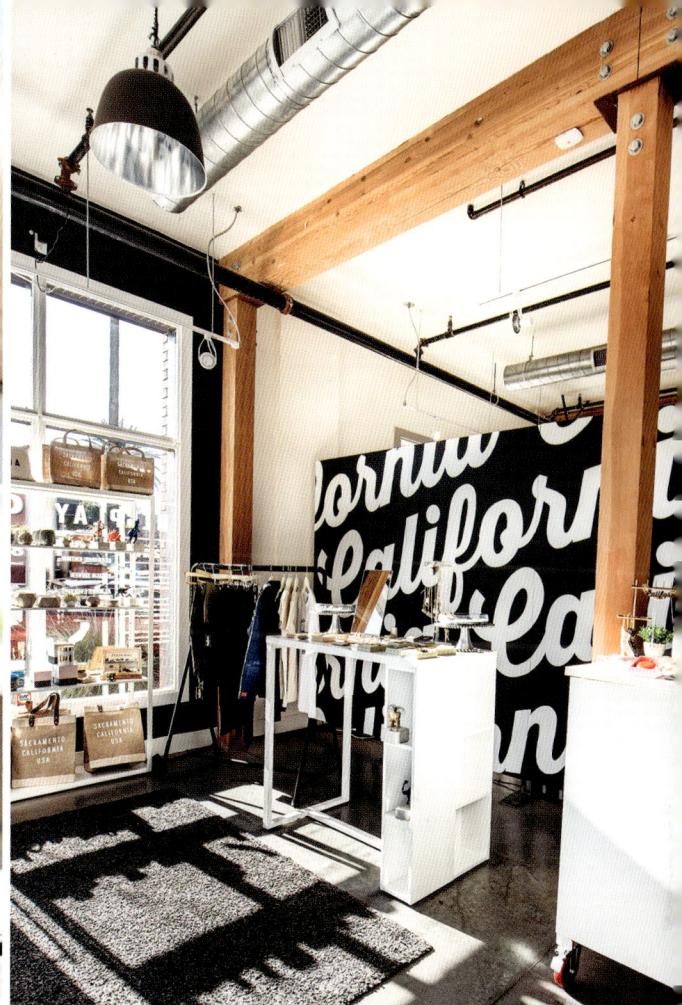

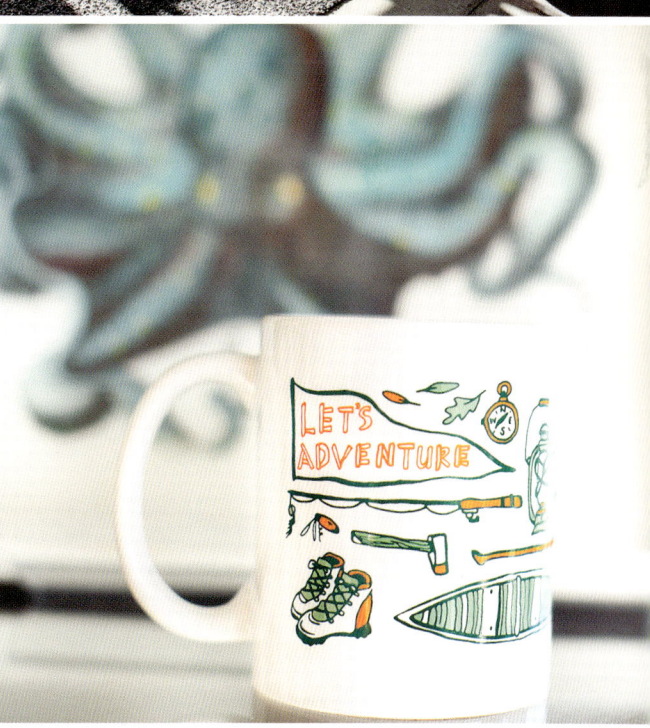

INSIDE *Oak Park*

# THE PLANT FOUNDRY

Oak Park might not seem an obvious location for a unique boutique that specializes in artisanal plants and flowers, but The Plant Foundry owner Angela Pratt is not a merchant who followed a familiar path to her success. From childhood, Pratt loved getting her hands dirty while digging in the dirt. Her mother took her to a local nursery for its calming influence and rewarded young Pratt with plants. That early exposure was never forgotten. After an education that included horticultural studies at American River College and UC Davis, Pratt's dream shop became a reality in December 2015, when she discovered the perfect Broadway location in a former filling station. The Plant Foundry specializes in edible and ornamental plants, artisan goods, organic gardening, quality tools, supplies and gifts. Driven by Pratt's dedication and deep roots in the nursery business, The Plant Foundry has blossomed.

3500 Broadway
916.917.5787
plantfoundry.com

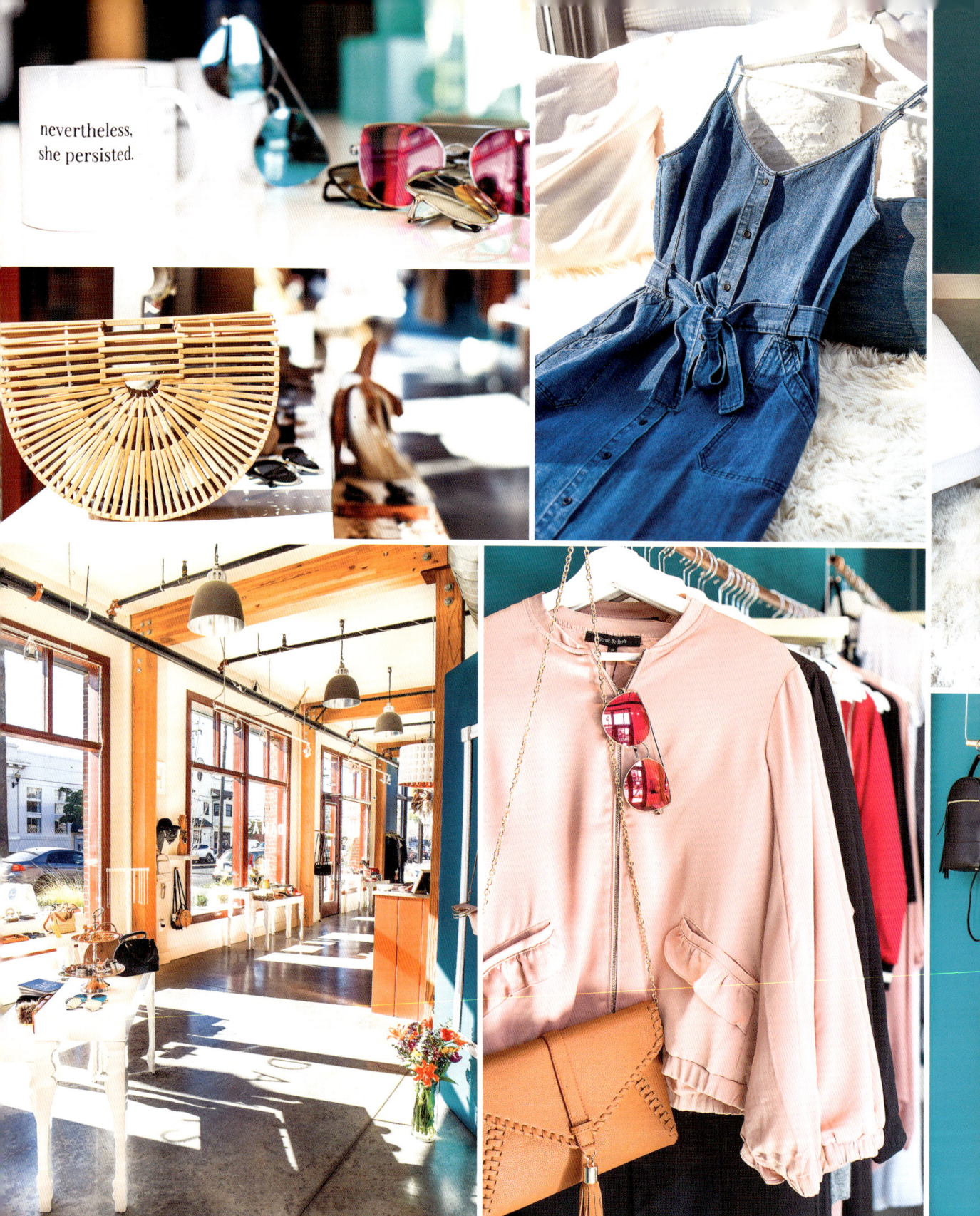

Inside *Oak Park*

# DAMAS

A unique environment for women entrepreneurs has arrived at 34th and Broadway in Oak Park. DAMAS seeks to build a platform for women to present, buy and sell clothing and accessories while sharing ideas and socializing. As the first "For Women By Women" retail concept store on the West Coast, DAMAS is a light-filled space featuring unique products, all created by women artisans and designers. Founders Maritza Davis (seated) and Anette Thomas located DAMAS next to Oak Park's original concept store, DISPLAY: California, which hosts rotating pop-up shops. The DAMAS experience comes complete with a social club. Events include trunk shows and talks that encourage local women to connect, learn and grow.

3417 Broadway
916.634.9005
ishopdamas.com

INSIDE *Oak Park*

# OAKHAUS

Tom Schnetz finds inspiration in diverse cultures and cuisines. After building his Oak Park taqueria, La Venadita, into a success, the restaurateur returned to his German roots with Oakhaus, a modern take on the hof brau. Mini corn dogs, "hausmade" pickles and homemade pretzels highlight the snack menu, followed by hearty offerings such as a pastrami and sauerkraut sandwich on house-made rye, sausages from V. Miller Meats served on a roll with potato salad, slow-roasted prime rib with horseradish cream, and sides like Grandma's stuffing and roasted cauliflower with Parmesan. The bar has 14 handles of beer and cider on tap and more than 50 options of bottled and canned beer. Oakhaus even has an off-premises beer license. Yes, unopened brews can be carted home.

**3413 Broadway
916.376.7694
oakhaussac.com**

INSIDE *Oak Park*

# LA VENADITA

With décor inspired by the artistry of Frida Kahlo's masterpiece "The Wounded Deer," this hotspot for creative Mexican food is a homecoming for restaurateur Thomas Schnetz and his brother and business partner, David. The Schnetzes grew up in Sacramento and opened their first restaurant locally before establishing a string of successful eateries in the Bay Area. La Venadita is the Oak Park culmination of their experience, featuring the authentic cuisine Thomas learned to prepare during his frequent trips to Mexico. The menu includes simple, tasty dishes such as crispy carnitas tacos, albondigas (meatball) tacos, enchiladas with mushrooms, asparagus and poblano cream, vegetarian chile relleno and combo plate classics. La Venadita means "little deer" and the restaurant's logo derived from Kahlo's self-portrait as a deer struggling to overcome fate. A full bar highlighted by tequila and mescal libations, including specialty margaritas, piña coladas and daiquiris, keeps customers refreshed and relaxed.

**3501 3rd Avenue**
**916.400.4676**
**lavenaditasac.com**

INSIDE *Oak Park*

## OLD SOUL CO.

Serendipity describes the concept of Old Soul Co. The owners, Tim Jordan and Jason Griest (shown), first met over coffee. Jordan was one of Griest's first customers when Griest opened Naked Coffeehouse in 2002. Four years later, these two talented men formalized their ideas for artisanal breads and coffee roasting into a business partnership that advanced Sacramento's reputation as one of the best independent and craft coffee cities in the United States. Today, Old Soul Co. has four local locations, all successful and true to the spirit of fresh coffee and breads in a pleasant urban environment. The original Old Soul Co. grew from the discovery of an obscure but charming former storage warehouse in an alley near 18th and L streets. Today, the old warehouse serves as the base of operations for the brand's roasting, baking and educational classes. Old Soul Co. sources coffee from Ethiopia, Mexico, Costa Rica, Nicaragua, Panama and Honduras. Fresh baked goods are created daily. The newest location on R Street features not only coffee, but a full-service restaurant and bar called Pullman—a salute to the historic corridor's legacy as the street where Theodore Judah engineered the West's first rail line in 1852. The bar features casual classics and craft cocktails.

**Old Soul @ 40 Acres**
3434 Broadway
916.483.8540
oldsoulco.com

**The Alley**
1716 L Street (rear alley)
916.443.7685

**Old Soul at The Weatherstone**
812 21st Street
196.443.6340

**555 Capital Mall**
916.890.1555

# UNDERGROUND BOOKS & GUILD THEATER

Underground Books doesn't simply serve its neighborhood. It reflects and embraces the neighborhood—a shop that celebrates the vibrancy of Oak Park. Founded in 2003 by the gregarious Mother Rose (a.k.a. owner Georgia West), the bookstore is the community's literacy headquarters, with author talks, book discussions, children's story time sessions and countless fun events. The shop serves as an adjunct to the Guild Theater next door, which frequently showcases films, lectures and live performances. The historic Guild Theater is the only remaining theater among several early-20th century movie houses for which Oak Park was once known, and it has been noted by Sacramento author Joan Didion as the place where she enjoyed European art films as a young woman. The Guild and Underground Books are integrated within the 23,000-square-foot 40 Acres Art Gallery and Cultural Center, which houses Old Soul Co. coffeehouse, apartments and rotating exhibitions that feature student and professional artists while chronicling Oak Park's history as the city's cultural hub.

2814 35th Street
916.737.3333
underground-books.com

2828 35th Street
916.905.7024
guildtheater.com

# VIBE HEALTH BAR

Clean, lean and healthy snacks are the point at Vibe Health Bar. Open since March 2016, Vibe's goal is to bring healthy food and drink options to the heart of the Broadway Triangle neighborhood in Oak Park. Açaí bowls are one specialty: "superfood" açaí berries mixed with organic ingredients such as coconut, local honey, granola, pineapple and bee pollen. Vibe features salads, sandwiches, wraps and unique smoothies. Notable is the "City of Trees," a blend of kale, pineapple, mango, jalapeño, basil, goji berry, ginger, coconut water and Himalayan salt, which Vibe owner Brandon Brodzky (shown behind bar) insists "tastes like sunshine." Brodzky and his business partner Blake Houston (at left) have redesigned the space to feel cozy like a coffee shop, with free wifi and room to relax. A mini art gallery featuring local artists enhances the walls. Vibe carries products from local purveyors, including Chocolate Fish Coffee, Brass Clover Cold Brew Coffee, Revive Kombucha and Zeal Kombucha, giving customers easy access to local, healthy food and drinks.

**3515 Broadway**
916.382.9723
vibehealthbar.com

**4601 H Street**
916.970.5102

# INSIDE *East Sac*

Cool boutiques, fabulous eateries, and craft coffeehouses and brew pubs encourage get-togethers in this close-knit community. McKinley Park not only has an award-winning classical rose garden, but also the city's largest and most interesting community-built playground.

Hike and bike the American River Parkway trail that borders family-friendly, mid-century River Park. Sac State's campus brings student energy spilling over into the city's original East Sac "Little Italy" enclave.

Stroll the leafy canopied streets of the Fab Forties and Elmhurst Parkway, and visit McKinley Park's charming duck pond. McKinley Village—East Sac's newest neighborhood—features delightful public art in its many new community parks. Shown at left is "La Feuille," a sculpture by Marc Foster.

Tahoe Park features affordable housing, new home developments, a budding retail scene and active families.

East Sac was President Ronald Reagan's home base when he was the state's governor.

INSIDE *East Sac*

# 33RD STREET BISTRO

Food inspired by the Pacific Northwest was a unique and winning restaurant concept in 1995, when brothers Fred (shown at left) and Matt Haines returned home to Sacramento from Portland and Seattle and opened 33rd Street Bistro. Two decades later, the brothers and their celebrated formula for success have gained iconic status in East Sacramento, where 33rd Street Bistro has established itself with extraordinary style, flavor and consistency. The sophisticated but casual eatery serves breakfast, lunch and dinner—along with a traditional happy hour that fills the bar and patio. The menu features fresh ingredients, generous portions and colorful presentations. Craft cocktails are a house specialty, and the wine list brings unique pairings with more than 40 wines from Washington, Oregon and California, all available by the glass. The Haines brothers have expanded their dining empire to include the Riverside Clubhouse in Land Park and Suzie Burger in Midtown. Their fine touch at 33rd Street Bistro remains true to the core.

3301 Folsom Boulevard
916.455.2233
33rdstreetbistro.com

INSIDE *East Sac*

# CHOCOLATE FISH COFFEE ROASTERS

Small-batch coffees brewed from beans harvested within the past 12 months are the rule at Chocolate Fish Coffee Roasters, where the bean is king. Founded in 2008 by husband and wife Andy and Edie Baker, Chocolate Fish Coffee takes its product to extremes. The Bakers and their coffee-loving team travel the world to bring the best beans back to Sacramento. Among the regular stops are Guatemala, Colombia, Costa Rica, Honduras and El Salvador. On the road, the Chocolate Fish crew builds personal relationships and tracks the integrity and sustainable farming practices of purveyors. The coffee beans that find their way to Sacramento have passed inspection for microclimates, quality assurance and care in handling. The Bakers even created Specialty Coffee Week to introduce more unique flavors. A "chocolate fish" is a New Zealand confection given as thanks for a good deed. The name reflects the result at Chocolate Fish Coffee Roasters.

**East Sacramento Café & Roastery**
**4749 Folsom Boulevard**
**916.451.5181**

**Downtown Coffee Bar**
**3rd and Q Streets**
**chocolatefishcoffee.com**

**Opening 2018**
**2940 Freeport Boulevard**
**Land Park**

INSIDE *East Sac*

# CORTI BROTHERS

Brothers Frank and Gino Corti opened their grocery store in 1947 to expand the culinary experiences of Sacramento residents. They offered delicacies and wines from around the world, not easily available in Northern California at the time. Frank's son, Darrell Corti (shown), continues the tradition in the quaint East Sacramento grocery store. Darrell's encyclopedic knowledge of food and wine led to the creation in 1967 of his legendary food newsletter, featuring products discovered on travels abroad. The letter is still published to ravenous readers across the country. Corti was knighted as a Cavaliere by the Italian government for his work in promoting Italian products. Today, America's top chefs seek his opinion on all matters culinary. The Corti team includes expert wine stewards and journeyman meat cutters, but the store retains the old-fashioned charm first envisioned by the Corti brothers. The full-service delicatessen is famous for sandwiches and ravioli, the oldest continuously produced food product in Sacramento. The selection of charcuterie and cheese is comprehensive, as is the stock of specialty food products from all over the world.

5810 Folsom Boulevard
916.736.3800
cortibrothers.com

INSIDE *East Sac*

# EAST SAC HARDWARE

Sheree Johnston is called "The Hardware Lady." Equal parts teacher, problem solver, business manager and team leader, Johnston owns East Sac Hardware with her husband, Rich (she is shown here with their son, Ricky). Sheree holds a master's degree in education and ran the local, independent hardware store's paint department in the late 1980s and early 1990s, so she's well qualified for her multiple tasks. The shop has served East Sacramento and the surrounding area since 1951 and features the essentials—tools, fasteners, plants, plumbing supplies, key cutting, tool sharpening, screen and lamp repair services and, naturally, paint—with a focus on products made in the U.S. The Hardware Lady conducts classes on the Amy Howard At Home One Step Paint system, antiquing, household repairs and general strategies for hands-on home improvement.

4800 Folsom Boulevard
916.457.7558
eastsachardware.com

INSIDE *East Sac*

## CANON EAST SACRAMENTO

A legacy of Michelin stars, music and artistic celebration provides the unlikely backdrop for a remarkable success story on 34th Street. Canon showcases the talent and imagination of owner Clay Nutting (shown at left) and chef Brad Cecchi. Nutting is a visionary on the Sacramento arts and dining scene, and Cecchi is one of the city's most skilled chefs, having worked at Mulvaney's, Grange and Solbar, a Michelin-starred resort restaurant in Calistoga. Canon is housed in a reimagined warehouse and based on the neighborhood pub concept—fine dining presented in a casual tavern atmosphere, complete with a full bar brimming with artisanal cocktails. The food gains inspiration from global cuisines, including Southeast Asian, North African and Latin American. The menu is hyper-seasonal with roots firmly planted in Northern California. All dishes are designed to be shared, even the tater tots with mole sauce.

**1719 34th Street**
**916.469.2433**
**canoneastsac.com**

INSIDE *East Sac*

# KERRIE KELLY DESIGN LAB

Interior designer and author Kerrie Kelly travels the world to discover the latest inspirations in sleek, approachable design. Her journeys reaffirm Kelly's belief that every home or workplace deserves a beautiful look, which reflects the mantra of her interior design business and East Sac design lab. An award-winning and certified interior designer with 20 years in the business and experience at every level, large and small, Kelly brings a precise, appropriate touch to any commercial or residential space. She specializes in bright, comfortable designs that aren't intimidated by luxury or beholden to trends. Kelly accommodates a variety of styles and preferences, from organic luxury living to reimagined classic designs brought to life with texture, color and light. In addition to helping Sacramento home and business owners achieve their dream interiors, Kelly judges student design competitions and launches product collaborations with international kitchen and bath companies. And she's a multimedia consultant for several national home furnishing brands. The Kerrie Kelly Design Lab offers retail accessories with a specialty in window coverings. The lab features more than 150 window treatment styles, all custom-made in the United States.

**5704 Elvas Avenue
916.706.2089
kerriekelly.com**

INSIDE *East Sac*

# #PANACHE

Parisian couture may not logically align with doorknobs, but surprising alignments are what makes #Panache a magical place at 53rd and H streets. Ralph Barnett and Hector Lopez run the store as an extension of their lives and a reflection of their personalities. The result is a treasure trove boutique, unique and forever changing. Lopez's passion has always been designer fashion—the Mexico native has collected vintage handbags, jewelry, sunglasses and footwear since 1994. Barnett's specialty is something he calls "mantiques," repurposed vintage furniture, wall hangings and conversation pieces such as religious artifacts. The pair opened #Panache in 2016 and comingled their collections into a one-stop shop for rare finds. Vintage Chanel and other European couture in stunning condition fills space alongside salutes to France, notably vintage Paris street signs and matchboxes adorned with the Eiffel Tower.

**5379 H Street**
**916.813.5758**

INSIDE *East Sac*

# McKINLEY PARK CENTER

Wedding receptions, parties and smaller gatherings find an elegant home in the Art Deco–era Grand Hall at East Sacramento's historic McKinley Park. With lovingly restored wood paneling and timber beams, the Grand Hall provides an inspirational setting for any event. The building and grounds are part of the Clunie Community Center, an updated 1930s facility run by the nonprofit Friends of East Sacramento. The center features four unique rental spaces for groups of 12 to 200 people, including kitchen facilities and a patio overlooking the park and swimming pool. A smaller rental room features an historic display of East Sacramento photographs. Friends of East Sacramento also manages the breathtakingly beautiful McKinley Rose Garden, the city's best, with 1,200 rose bushes, eight companion perennial beds and a wrought iron gazebo. Rental rates are very affordable at this popular venue, maintained by a group of dedicated volunteers who keep the gardens perfectly manicured within the timeless and historic setting.

Alhambra Boulevard and H Street
916.243.8292
mckinleyparkcenter.org

INSIDE *East Sac*

## ONESPEED

Sausage, tomatoes, potatoes, caramelized onions, olives and goat cheese provide essential sustenance at OneSpeed, a self-described "neighborhood pizza joint" whose ambition belies the name. Opened in 2009 and crafted around a bicycle theme, OneSpeed is a casual but sophisticated counterpoint to owner Rick Mahan's superb Midtown restaurant, The Waterboy. OneSpeed celebrates fresh and locally sourced ingredients and conjures simple flavors from dishes Mahan calls "seasonally relevant." The pizzas are a joy, from the healthy garden pie to the meaty sausage pie. Options run deep at OneSpeed. Antipasto and spaghetti pomodoro represent classic fare. There's even a burger, with a homemade bun stacked high with sautéed onions, peppers, white cheddar and rosemary mayonnaise.

**4818 Folsom Boulevard**
**916.706.1748**
**onespeedpizza.com**

INSIDE *East Sac*

# OBO' ITALIAN TABLE & BAR

OBO' draws inspiration from the simple, nourishing flavors and seasonal cooking traditions of rural Italy. The food is hearty and artisanal, served in a historic brick building that features a full bar, with patio seating along Seville Way at the corner of Folsom Boulevard. The latest addition to Selland Family Restaurants, OBO' delivers monthly specials and café delights that include hot and cold sandwiches, wood-fired pizzas, hot entrees from saltimbocca to pot roast, pastas, and cold salad sides, as well as soups and focaccia. Meats are roasted to perfection. The pasta is homemade. Guests can enjoy a glass of wine, craft beers from local brewers or a cocktail from the bar—including 12 house specialties.

**3145 Folsom Boulevard**
**916.822.8720**
**oboitalian.com**

INSIDE *East Sac*

# THE KITCHEN RESTAURANT

For 25 years, The Kitchen has been the ultimate dining destination for the Sacramento region and beyond. Innovative and unmatched for pure culinary enjoyment and genuine hospitality, The Kitchen serves a five-course prix fixe seasonal dinner menu featuring the best and freshest ingredients available, mostly procured locally and regionally. The executive chef and staff present the menu in a lively, theatrical demonstration format. Guests are invited to stroll throughout the open kitchen, chat with the chefs, visit the wine cellar and relax on the patio. Husband-and-wife chefs Randall Selland and Nancy Zimmer, along with their grown children, Josh Nelson and Tamera Baker, founded The Kitchen Restaurant in 1991. The Selland family was among the first to emphasize farm-to-fork dining in the Sacramento region. The quality, commitment, and passion that the Selland family brings to The Kitchen have created a landmark restaurant that has sold out nightly since its inception. The Kitchen Restaurant has earned every imaginable local and regional award along with an impressive list of national accolades, including the AAA Five Diamond Award six years running, a nod as a semi-finalist for the James Beard "Outstanding Restaurant" Award, the highest Zagat ratings, and honors from *Wine Spectator* and *Wine Enthusiast*, as well as inclusion in the Yelp Top 100 and the Open Table Top 100.

2225 Hurley Way
916.568.7171
thekitchenrestaurant.com

Inside *East Sac*

# TWIGGS FLORAL DESIGN

Twiggs is not an average florist. As an international buyer and award-winning floral designer, owner Wes Green travels the world to gather ideas and inspiration for his unique floral creations and home accessories. Twiggs Floral Design specializes in breathtaking arrangements for any occasion for individual or corporate clients. Green and his design team hand-select and import fresh, premium flowers and botanicals daily. Arrangements demonstrate a variety of creative floral design styles to emphasize complementary or monochromatic color palettes, natural elements, plus multiple textures and botanical groupings. The Twiggs signature style follows the European aesthetic: clean, elemental and architectural, with a combination of function, fashion and form. Stunning plantscapes are the result. The tiny storefront tucked into a cluster of shops bursts with elegant décor items, glassware, candles and flora and gives Twiggs Floral Design the appearance of an enchanted apothecary brimming with nature's bounty.

3250 J Street
916.441.2302
twiggsfloraldesign.com

INSIDE East Sac

# SELLAND'S MARKET-CAFÉ

Selland's Market-Café is a casual, family-friendly neighborhood café in East Sac preparing handcrafted, quality seasonal foods. Selland's offers a wide array of menu options including wood-fired pizzas, sandwiches, fresh salads, hot and cold prepared foods from the deli cases, soups, seasonal specials and house-made desserts. At Selland's, guests can enjoy boutique and local wines by the glass and bottle, as well as craft beers and kombucha on tap. Selland's is a neighborhood institution with something for everyone. Established in 2001, Selland's Market-Café is family owned and operated by Selland Family Restaurants co-founders, chefs Randall Selland and Nancy Zimmer and their grown children, Josh Nelson and Tamera Baker. The Selland family also owns acclaimed local restaurants The Kitchen, Ella Dining Room & Bar and OBO' Italian Table & Bar. The Selland family has provided high-quality dining experiences using products and ingredients sourced largely from local producers and the area's farmers markets for more than 25 years.

5340 H Street
916.736.3333
sellands.com

INSIDE *East Sac*

## KRU CONTEMPORARY JAPANESE CUISINE

Raw and refined, traditional and innovative, an inspired fusion of Asian, European and American ingredients and cooking techniques—such is the daily routine at Kru Contemporary Japanese Cuisine. Owner and chef Buu "Billy" Ngo (shown in hat) is the creative guide behind Kru's visually stunning and delicious dishes. He's a foodie celebrity, with appearances on culinary TV shows such as "Glutton for Punishment," "Man Fire Food" and "Cutthroat Kitchen." The chef was born in Hong Kong and moved to Sacramento as a baby. Kru started small, but today the restaurant is celebrated as the city's chicest sushi provider, with plates that please eye and palate. The menu features traditional classics, including wakame (seaweed) salad, house-made pork gyoza, shrimp and vegetable tempura, chicken teriyaki, and pork belly and sea urchin uni served with teriyaki, arare and chili oil powder. Kru—the name is derived from the French word *cru*, or raw—also specializes in classics such as hamachi carpaccio, nigiri, sashimi and an array of sushi and hand rolls almost too beautiful to eat.

3135 Folsom Boulevard
916.551.1559
krurestaurant.com

INSIDE *East Sac*

# 57TH STREET ANTIQUE & DESIGN CENTER

A mixture of sophisticated interior and exterior furnishings and design, food, spa services and antiques beckons at 57th Street Antique & Design Center. Called "the best-kept secret in Sacramento" by owner Gary Little, the 40,000-square-foot, multi-building historic complex near Elvas Avenue between H and J streets has established itself among the city's most eclectic centers, offering an acre of parking. Today the center includes retail gift and curated antique shops, full-service interior designers, a cross-training gym, a salon and spa, and an award-winning family restaurant run by chef Evan Elsberry. Evan's Kitchen and Catering is open for all three meals Tuesday through Saturday and for breakfast and lunch on Sundays. The popular eatery also offers notable winemaker dinners throughout the year. Stunning specialty shops showcasing original home designs and emerging décor trends mingle with antique shops of exceptional quality and style. Spend an hour or an entire day exploring the center's many treasures and experiences.

**855 57th Street**
**57thstreetantiquerow.com**

**Evan's Kitchen and Catering**
**916.452.3896**
**chefevan.com**

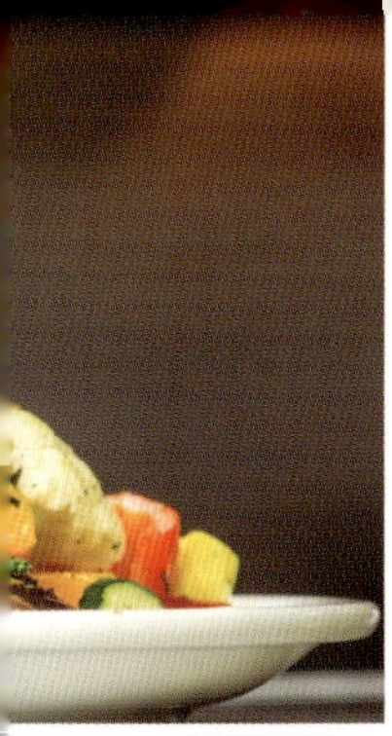

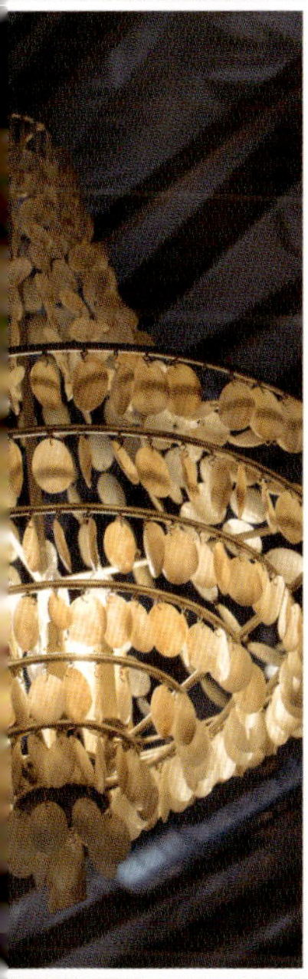

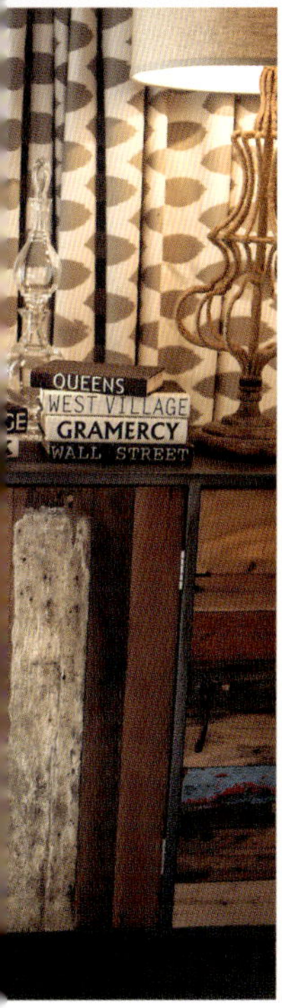
QUEENS
WEST VILLAGE
GRAMERCY
WALL STREET

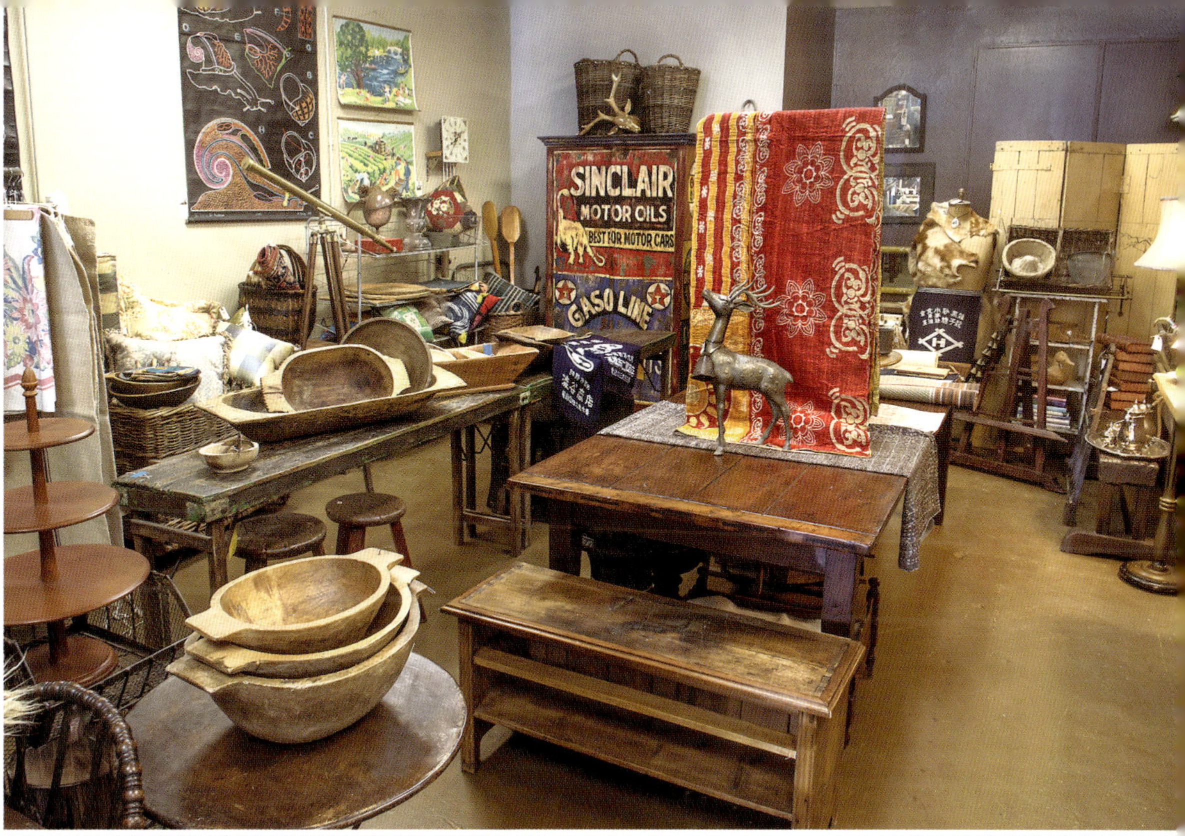
SINCLAIR
MOTOR OILS
BEST FOR MOTOR CARS
GASOLINE

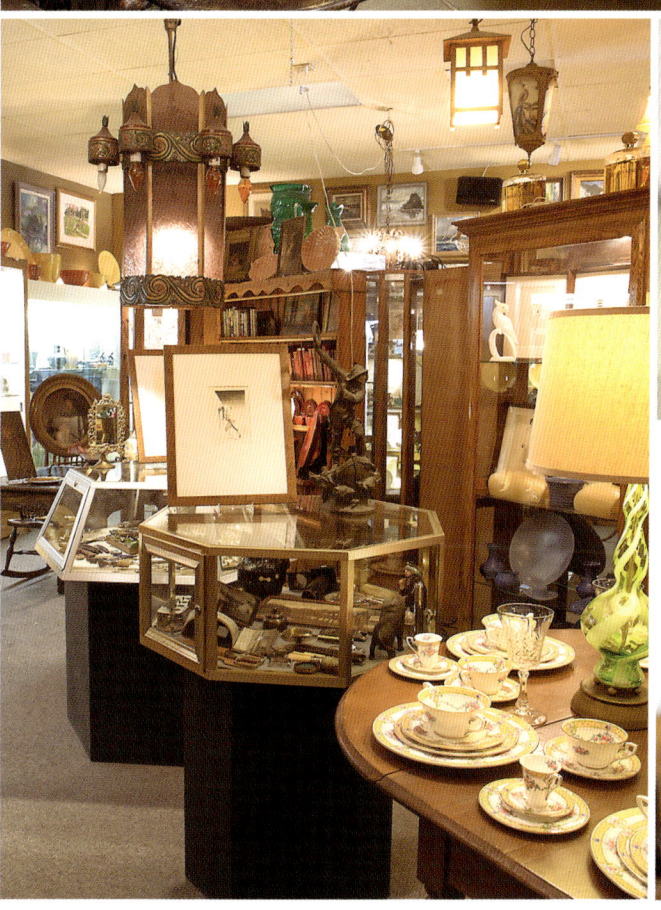

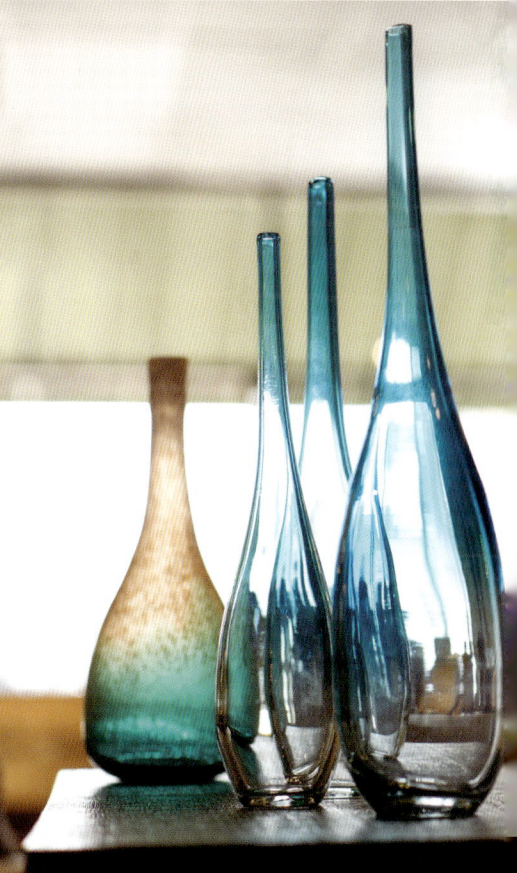

# OPA! OPA!

Phil Courey was raised on the classic Mediterranean dishes he features in his lively and colorful East Sacramento neighborhood restaurant. Opa! Opa! delivers the spirit, variety and freshness of Greek dining with dishes that highlight roasted lamb and marinated chicken, yogurt, spinach, cucumbers, olives and feta cheese. House specialties include spanakopita with feta and spinach, and dolmathes—the delicacy of stuffed grape leaves ubiquitous in the Mediterranean. Another traditional Greek favorite is gyro—spiced and tender, with a dip of tzatziki, carved from a cone of beef and lamb. The restaurant has a companion dessert shop called Sweeties, where classic baklava is served along with cupcakes, bars and cappuccinos.

**5644 J Street**
**916.451.4000**
**eatatopa.com**

# NOPALITOS SOUTHWESTERN CAFÉ

Southwestern cooking is a savory family affair at Nopalitos Southwestern Café, where husband and wife owners Dave and Rose Hanke (shown at right) share duties in the kitchen and front of the house. Opened in 1992 and packed with customers ever since, Nopalitos takes its name from the nopal cactus, a staple in Mexican kitchens beloved for its versatility and light, tangy flavor. The Hankes are masters of nopal cooking and coax delicious, understated magic from the edible, elongated cactus pads. Dave typically works the stove, while Rose bakes, serves dishes and maintains the restaurant's books. Nopalitos devotees arrive early for chile verde, chile colorado, smothered burrito, vegetarian Nopalitos quesadilla with roasted poblano chilies, along with traditional tamales, tostadas and tacos. As befits its home-style provenance, Nopalitos maintains quirky hours—the doors are open only for breakfast and lunch, and the kitchen closes on weekends.

**5530 H Street**
**916.452.8226**
nopalitoscafe.com

INSIDE *East Sac*

## HAWKS PROVISIONS & PUBLIC HOUSE

White subway tiles, gleaming glass and chrome, warm woods, deep teal walls and bar stools that look like vintage office chairs introduce a European flair to Alhambra Boulevard in the newest restaurant project from Molly Hawks and Michael Fagnoni. Acclaimed for Hawks, their fine-dining flagship in Granite Bay, the wife and husband team has taken a more informal approach to their urban destination. Public House features a menu filled with the best ingredients from small farms and local purveyors. Familiar classics get special treatment at Public House. The burger is made with house-ground Wagyu beef. Spaghetti becomes a delicacy with slow-roasted mushrooms. And the country paté with Armagnac-soaked prunes is a delicious twist on simplicity. Next door, Provisions provides take-out options, with house-made pastries, quiche and croque monsieur sandwiches, along with daily sandwich specials. Public House fulfills the expectations of its name with a full bar, where customers enjoy craft cocktails, local beer and a convivial environment.

**1525 Alhambra Boulevard**
**916.588.4440**
**hawkspublichouse.com**

## V. MILLER MEATS

Traditional butcher shops are rare finds, but a shop that specializes in 100 percent whole animal butchering is unique – which makes V. Miller Meats a remarkable homage to the meat cutter's art. Owner and butcher Eric Veldman Miller, who owns the shop with fellow chef Matt Azevedo, became interested in the craft of whole animal butchery while apprenticing under Master Butcher Terry Regassa. Previously, Miller built his culinary reputation as a chef at fine dining restaurants across the region, including Mulvaney's Building and Loan in Midtown. Recognizing the connections among local farmers, natural pastures and animal welfare as integral parts of the butchering process, Miller elected to operate a craft butchery and carry only high quality, pasture-raised and grass-fed meats. The V. Miller cold case contains pasture-raised beef, pork and lamb, free-range chicken, fresh sausage, cured meats and charcuterie, plus delectable deli meats, bone broth and stock. Head butcher Cindy Garcia makes an art of trimming the perfect cuts.

4801 Folsom Boulevard #2
916.400.4127
vmillermeats.com

INSIDE *East Sac*

## ALLORA

Elizabeth-Rose Mandalou, who owns Allora with her husband, chef Deneb Williams, recently jumped at the chance to open a restaurant after a popular family of florists retired and vacated their elegant contemporary brick building. Allora is definitely fine dining at its best. The Italian-inspired dishes are artistic and architectural in their beauty, sophisticated in their flavors and jewel-like in their proportions. The menu focuses on seafood, like the deceptively complex Insalata di Mare that jumbles together cold shrimp, calamari, crab and mussels, all perfectly cooked, seasoned and served with a stunningly beautiful salad of shaved asparagus and pea tendrils. Almost every dish is finished with flowers to pay tribute to the original family that built the space. A small but diverse selection of pastas, all house-made, highlights the kitchen's impressive skills without showboating. Mandalou, an advanced sommelier, opts for a noteworthy selection of varietals from California, Italy and beyond to stand up to the onslaught of elegance and sensations. It's no surprise that this is Williams and Mandalou's third restaurant. Allora shows a steady hand and wealth of experience. We all hope that this impressive couple will help keep Sacramento in the national culinary conversation for years to come.

**5215 Folsom Boulevard**
**916.538.6434**
allorasacramento.com

# INDEX OF PLACES

33rd Street Bistro (AK), 168-169
57th Street Antique Center (AK), 196-197
Allspicery, (AK), 25
Andy's Candy Apothecary (AK), 20-21
Art Galleries, 8-9
Art of Toys (AK), 124
Artists' Collaborative Gallery (AK), 60–61
Allora (LS), 204-205
Barn, The, 54-55
Benjamins Shoes (AK), 64-65
Biba Ristorante Italiano (RV), 94-95
Block Butcher Bar (RV), 98-99
Café Bernardo, 70–72
Cafeteria 15L (RV), 30-31
Canon East Sacramento (AK), 176-177
Casa Garden Restaurant (AK), 143
Centro Cocina Mexicana, 80–82
Chocolate Fish Coffee (AK), 33, 170-171
Corti Brothers (RV), 172-173
Crocker Art Museum (AK), 22-24
Damas (AK), 156-157
deVere's Irish Pub (RV), 34-35
DISPLAY: California (AK), 152-153
Downtown & Vine (RV), 32
East Sac Hardware (AK), 174-175
Ella Dining Room & Bar (RV), 36-37
Esquire Grill, 26-27
Fairytale Town (LS), 132-133
Federalist Public House (AK), 96-97
Firehouse Restaurant, The (RV), 58–59
Firestone Public House (RV), 38-39
Fish Face Poke Bar (AK), 73
Fleet Feet (RV), 82-83
Frank Fat's (RV), 40-41
Freeport Bakery (AK), 136-137
Ginger Elizabeth Chocolates (RV), 120-121
Grange Restaururant & Bar (AK), 28-29
Haberdasherie (AK) 108-109
Hawks Provisions & Public House (RV), 200-201
Historic Rose Garden, 142
Hook & Ladder Manufacturing Company (RV) 68-69
Hot Italian (RV), 46-47
Iron Grill (AK), 148
Iron Horse Tavern (LS), 74–75
Kerrie Kelly Design Lab (AK), 178-179
Kitchen Restaurant, The (RV), 188-189
Kru (RV), 194-195
La Venadita (AK), 160-161
La Cosecha (RV), 51
Lady Bird: The Movie (AK), 10-11
Localis (RV), 66-67
Lowbrau (RV), 110-111
Lumens Light & Living (AK), 100-101

Ma Jong's Asian Diner (RV), 42-43
Mayahuel (RV), 50
Magpie Café (RV), 72
McKinley Park Center, 182-183
Medium Rare & Kicksville (AK) 77
Midtown Farmers Market, 105
Mulvaney's Building & Loan (RV), 126-127
Murals (AK), 14-15
Nopalitos Southwestern Café (LS), 199
Oakhaus (LS) 158-159
OBO' Italian Table & Bar, 188-189
Old Soul Co. (AK), 162-163
OneSpeed (AK), 184-185
Opa! Opa! (LS), 198
#Panache (AK), 180-181
Paragary's, 84-85
Performing Arts, 12-13
Plant Foundry, The, 154-155
Preservation & Co. (AK), 48
Public Art, 104
Red Rabbit Kitchen & Bar, The (RV), 102-103
Revolution Wines (AK), 114
Rind, The (AK), 125
Rio City Café (RV), 56-57
Riverside Clubhouse (AK), 138-139
Sacramento Natural Foods Co-op, 86-87
Sacramento Zoo (LS), 134-135
Scout Living (AK), 122-123
Selland's Market-Café, 146-147, 192–193
Shoki Ramen House (AK), 76
Skool Japanese Gastropub (LS), 112-113
Soloman's Delicatessen, 45
South, 44
Sun & Soil Juice Company (AK), 87
Suzie Burger (AK), 86
Tapa the World (RV), 106-107
Taylor's Market & Kitchen (RV), 140-141
Temple Coffee Roasters (AK), 116-117
Time Tested Books (AK), 49
TRUE (AK), 114
Twiggs Floral Design (AK), 190-191
Underground Books & Guild Theater (AK), 164
University Art (AK), 90-91
V. Miller Meats (RV), 202-203
Vibe Health Bar (AK), 165
Vic's Ice Cream (AK), 144–145
Walk of Stars, Sacramento, 16-17
Waterboy, The (AK), 92-93
Willie's Burgers (AK), 148
Zocalo (AK), 128-129

Photographer Key: AK – Aniko Kiezel @anikophotos, RV – Rachel Valley @ rachelvalley, LS – Linda Smolek

# ACKNOWLEDGMENTS

Creating a book like this takes a very talented team. I am blessed to have one. The fabulous work of our photographers, Aniko Kiezel and Rachel Valley, speaks for itself on every page. Jessica Laskey wrote the book and managed the numerous details it took to pull off this enormous effort.

Graphic designer Brian Burch helped guide me in creating this beautiful book design. Longtime book publisher Helen Sweetland, now of Left Coast Book Works here in Sacramento, was invaluable in helping me negotiate the world of book publishing, printing and distribution. And I am grateful to Bob Graswich for contributing his expert editing skills.

My husband, Jim, deserves a great deal of love and credit for keeping our business and home life running smoothly while I took nearly a year away from both to create this book. And I am very grateful to my publication staff members Daniel Nardinelli, Cindy Fuller, Serena Marzion, Michael McFarland, Marybeth Bizjak, Linda Smolek, Lisa Schmidt and Lauren Hastings, who contributed design, photography, editing, distributing or web skills.

I am grateful to the small-business owners who welcomed us into their places, shared their stories with us and helped us with book sales.

There are a substantial number of compelling places in the city that are located beyond our selected neighborhoods. We found other businesses that we loved but that didn't work well for the book's photo format. And, unfortunately, a handful of great places that we wanted to include were not available for photography for a variety of reasons.

Finally, please know that this book is a snapshot of information on the day we went to press. Please visit insidesacbook.com and the individual business websites for updates.

And I want to give a thank you to our generous sponsors:

### Visit Sacramento
### Fulcrum Property

East Sacramento Chamber of Commerce
Rita Gibson Financial Services
Golden Pacific Bank
Bardis Homes
Sacramento State University
Downtown Sacramento Partnership
Dunnigan Realtors
McKinley Village by The New Home Company

Midtown Association & Sutter District
Oak Park Business Association
Sacramento Metro Chamber of Commerce
Sacramento Natural Foods Co-op
City Council Member Steve Hansen
City Council Member Jeff Harris
River City Bank
Tina Thomas
Marcy Friedman

# PHOTO AND DESIGN CREDITS

Front Cover: Thaddeus Thompson @thadtphotography (city), Aniko Kiezel (Crocker and vessel), Rachel Valley (burger).
Back Cover: Aniko Kiezel
Map Design: Daniel Nardinelli

Other photo credits include the Old Sac intro (page 52) with Delta Queen boat photo by Elizabeth Delgado @elzbth, all others are by Aniko Kiezel. Historic Rose Garden (page 142) the top middle photo by Dean Sonneborn, bottom left photo by Miranda Saake, and bottom right photo by Debby Sprigg. Land Park intro (page 130) and East Sac intro (page 166) include photo contributions by Steve Harriman. McKinley Park Center pages (page 182-183) top middle photo by Dean Sonneborn, bottom left photo by Miranda Saake, bottom right photo by Debby Sprigg, bottom left photo is by Mary Gray and the bottom right photo is by Shay Pang. All were honored winners in the McKinley Rose Garden's annual photo contest sponsored by Friends of East Sacramento.